P. 107 Schoenhut Trinity Chimes - 1904
P. " " piano - 19 c.
P. 145 Merry Makers Mouse Orchestra
P. 23 Fur mech. rabbit - violin
P. 24 Fur " knitting cat - 1870
P. 51 ala. Coon jigger - 1914
P. 58 Sand toy
P. 62 Spinning tops
P. 67 sleigh doll
P 87 Schoenhut Teddy
P 94 typewriter

P. 104 marotte
P 112 Schoenhut
circus

Mechanical Toys

Mechanical Toys

Charles Bartholomew

Introduction by
Harriet Bridgeman

CHARTWELL BOOKS INC.

Acknowledgements

Bergström and Boyle Books, London: 58, 99, 134/Top and Bottom, 138/Bottom, 139/Top and Bottom, 142/Top and Bottom, 143/Bottom, 146–147; Bowes Museum, Barnard Castle: 15, 22/Top; Castle Museum, York: 56, 95/Bottom; Christie's, South Kensington: 23/Bottom, 25/Top, 43/Bottom, 45/Bottom, 48/Bottom, 53/Top Right, 57/Bottom Left, 85/Right, 137/Top, 144/Bottom, 145/Bottom; Constance Eileen King: 104, 105/Left, 148; Cooper-Bridgeman Library: 14, 18, 19, 23/Top, 26, 27/Top, 29/Top, 30/Top and Bottom, 31, 32/Top, 34, 35/Centre and Bottom, 37/Top and Bottom, 38, 39/Bottom, 41/Bottom, 42, 44/Top and Bottom, 50, 51/Top and Bottom Right, 52, 59/Left and Right, 61/Top and Bottom, 62/Top, 63, 65/Top and Bottom, 66, 67/Top, 68, 69/Top Left, Top Right, Left and Bottom, 71/Bottom, 73/Bottom, 80/Top, 89/Top, 92/Top, 93/Bottom, 96/Top, 100/Top and Bottom, 107/Top, 109/Top and Bottom, 112/Right, 114, 117, 119/Bottom, 122/Top, 129, 132/Top and Bottom, 135/Top, 138/Top, 140/Bottom; Ken Jackson, London: 53/Bottom, 64/Bottom, 72, 73/Top, 76/Top Left, 77/Top, 85/Left, 96/Bottom, 98/Top, 101, 121/Top, 133, 136; Margaret Woodbury Strong Museum, Rochester: 47, 67/Bottom, 70/Top and Bottom, 71/Top, 82/Bottom, 83/Top and Bottom, 87/Bottom, 107/Bottom, 115/Top; Mary Evans Picture Library, London: 102/Bottom; Mary Hillier: 10, 11, 12/Left and Right, 13/Top and Bottom, 16, 17/Top and Bottom, 22/Bottom, 25/Bottom, 27/Bottom, 32/Bottom, 40/Right, 43/Top, 48/Top Left, Centre, and Right, 53/Top Left, 54, 75, 76/Top Right, 80/Bottom, 81/Bottom, 84/Right, 88/Right, 89/Bottom, 90/Top Left, Top Right, Centre, and Bottom, 105/Right, 112/Left, 115/Bottom; Munro/Deighton, London: 149; Museum of London: 21/Left and Right, 51/Bottom Left, 57/Bottom Right, 60, 82/Top, 86, 108, 125/Centre and Bottom, 130/Top; Norfolk Museums' Service: 91, 102/Top; Radio Times Hulton Picture Library: 20/Bottom, 22/Centre, 45/Top, 97/Top and Bottom, 98/Bottom; Science Museum, London: 116/Left and Right, 118, 122/Bottom, 124/Top and Bottom, 125/Top, 126/Top and Bottom; Sotheby's, Belgravia: 33/Top and Bottom, 36/Top and Bottom, 39/Top, 55, 88/Left, 92/Bottom, 93/Right, 103/Top, 113/Top and Bottom, 128, 137/Bottom, 140/Top, 141, 144/Top; Tunbridge Wells Museum: 24/Bottom; Victoria and Albert Museum, London: 20/Top, 24/Top, 28, 29/Bottom, 35/Top and Bottom, 40/Left, 41/Top, 44/Middle, 46, 49/Top and Bottom, 57/Top, 62/Bottom, 64/Top, 74, 78, 79, 87/Top, 94 Right and Left, 95/Top, 103/Bottom, 106, 110, 111, 119/Top, 120, 121/Bottom, 123, 127, 130/Bottom, 131/Top and Bottom, 135/Bottom, 143/Top; Worthing Museum and Art Gallery: 77/Bottom, 81/Top.

Special thanks to Roger and Chris Church; Stuart and Linda Copper; Caroline Goodfellow (of the Bethnal Green Museum); Hilary Kay and Patricia Sherston (of Sotheby's, Belgravia); Mary Hillier; Patrick Rylands; Brian Webb; and Margaret and Blair Whitton (of the Margaret Woodbury Strong Museum, Rochester, N.Y.) for their extremely generous help and advice. And, last, but not least, many thanks to Charlotte Parry-Crooke for organizing all the photographs, and for sharing her expertise.

Endpapers and title page: photographs by Iain Reid.

Published by Chartwell Books Inc.,
A Division of Book Sales Inc.,
1000 Enterprise Ave., Secausus,
New Jersey 07094

Copyright © The Hamlyn Publishing Group Limited, 1979
ISBN 0 89009-273-7

Phototypeset by Keyspools Limited, Golborne, Lancs.

Color separations by Vidicolour Limited, Hemel Hempstead, Herts.

Printed in Madrid, Spain
by Mateu Cromo

Library of Congress catalog card number: 78-71450

Contents

Introduction

Toys have often given as much pleasure to those adults who made them as to those children who played with them, and in no respect can this be truer than in the field of mechanical toys.

In the past mechanical toys have often been made on such an ambitious scale and to suit such sophisticated whims that the delicacy of their mechanisms could fit them for handling by an adult only, but, equally, these lifelike miniature versions of elements in the adult world have provided children with an endless source of entertainment.

FIG. 33
THÉORÈME XI DE HÉRON D'ALEXANDRIE
(d'après Aleotti)

FIG. 35
THÉORÈME XI DE HÉRON D'ALEXANDRIE
(d'après Aleotti)

FIG. 34
THÉORÈME XXXVII DE HÉRON D'ALEXANDRIE
(d'après Aleotti)

FIG. 36
THÉORÈME LIV DE HÉRON D'ALEXANDRIE
(d'après Aleotti)

Hero of Alexandria's designs and diagrams for automata. From *Aleotti Gli artificiosi et curiosi moti spirituali di Herrone*, Ferrara, 1589.

The tradition of mechanical science dates back to classical times. Homer made one of the earliest references to mysterious self-motivating machines, alluding to the life-sized golden hand maidens of Hephaistos:

To whose feet little wheels of gold
*   he put, to go withal*
And enter his rich dining room alone,
*   their motion free*
And back again go out alone,
*   miraculous to see. (Illiad. Book 18)*

Like Homer, Plato also referred to mythical characters who made mechanised figures of the gods. Daedalus, he said, incorporated quicksilver into his creations which, 'unless they were fastened they would of themselves run away'. But it is not unlikely that Plato had actually seen such wonders. A contemporary of his, Archytas of Tarentum, the celebrated Pythagoran philosopher, cosmographer and mechanician, is reputed to have invented a wooden pigeon that could fly but could not rise again once it had settled. Present-day experts such as Mary Hillier, consider that Archytas's invention was worked by means of weights and compressed air.

Another early inventor of automata was Hero of Alexandria (285–222 B.C.). In his treatise on the subject, the *Epeiritalia*, Hero described a fascinating diversity of experiments connected with the making of toys, extending from the purely scientific to the notably frivolous. His earliest success was with a singing bird whose mechanism, similar to that of the modern bird-warbler whistle, worked by means of air pressure on water. Hero also invented other toys activated by water including a complex arrangement of four small birds watching an owl: the birds began to sing as soon as the owl's back was turned but ceased the minute he turned to face them again. Another of these toys consisted of a pedestal holding four small bushes, each with a bird on one of its branches. When water was released into the funnel, the first bird began to whistle, followed by the second, third and fourth and back to the first. Apart from experiments with water, Hero also used heat to increase air pressure, thus motivating certain mechanical and automatic devices. One of the best examples of his ingenuity in this respect was an altar on which two figures offered libations to the sacrifice. When the fire on the altar, which was constructed in the form of an airtight metal box, was lit, the air in the altar expanded, forcing liquid through the central tube within the box and down tubes running through the body and the right arm of each figure.

Although Hero produced an unrivalled wealth of ideas, they were to lie dormant in the western world for over a thousand years. The first Latin edition of his *Epeiritalia* was published by Corumardinus in Italy in 1575, and in the same century Baldi, the mathematician, applied some of Hero's hydraulic principles to the construction of mechanical figures and to making a toy eagle fly. Over three hundred years later interest was still sufficiently active for a Frenchman, Poyot, to reconstruct some of his models.

With the development of clockwork movements, worked by means of heavy weights and pulleys, the development of mechanical figures took a decisive turn. From the fourteenth century onwards, records exist of mechanical figures known as Jacquemarts, or Jacks, a type of clock which struck a bell each hour of the day. Some of the earliest examples of this type were made in the form of a soldier in armour, a reminder of the days when guards kept watch in order to raise the alarm, but this uniform was soon replaced by variations, and the soldier was replaced by mythological and classical figures such as Vulcan and Hercules. Turret clocks, often designed with no clockface, are also recorded as having operated in a few English church towers by 1400. These struck at the hour as

Zytglogge, a clock with automata made in Berne, Switzerland in 1530.

well, but also played a tune every three.

At the same time in Europe, primitive forms of automata were also used to demonstrate the principles of Christianity. Mechanical figures, devised so that a preacher could operate them from his pulpit with a foot pedal, reproduced the effect of the Crucifixion on a carved wooden figure of Christ, or brought to life the spectacle of the Virgin and Child. In general, however, the Church was suspicious of anything mechanical, thinking it too closely resembled pagan magic (St. Thomas Aquinas, for one, is known to have spoken out against it), but the folk festivals of the Middle Ages were not to be so easily silenced. Ambitious and beautifully designed automata continued to be displayed at these social gatherings, and gradually a new intellectual attitude prompted by the Reformation and the Counter-Reformation, tempered extremist values and allowed mechanical developments to reach new heights. Leonardo da Vinci, the great scientist and artist, invented a few mechanical toys, but it was not Italy but Germany, particularly Augsburg and Nuremberg, with their concentrations of skilled metalsmiths for armour and gun-making, which became an important manufacturing centre for mechanical toys and clocks in the sixteenth century, and which produced some truly phenomenal creations at the end of the seventeenth and the beginning of the eighteenth centuries.

As was the case with Da Vinci and others in his time and before, the master craftsmen and their workers in these areas had to rely on support from the court and the nobility since materials were very expensive and since mechanical inventions took a long time to produce. This patronage enabled the craftsmen to experiment with purely decorative and non-functional automata and to come up with new inventions such as the spring-driven clock. It is not known where or at what time this mechanism was first tried out, but, as it enabled craftsmen to make portable clocks for the first

Above
The Passion Clock, Augsburg. *c.* 1580. Abeler Museum, Wuppertal.

Right
Neptune riding mechanical tortoise. South German. Early 17th cent. Length: 27 cm (10.8 in). Victoria and Albert Museum, London.

Left
Cupid riding on a gold and silver
moving cart with clock. Made by
Andreas Stahel of Augsburg c. 1600.
Length: 30.5 cm (12.2 in). Badisches
Landesmuseum, Karlsruhe.

Below
Wooden clockwork man with moving
eyes and mouth. German. 18th cent.
Height: 59 cm (23.6 in). Abeler
Museum, Wuppertal.

time, it revolutionized the industry and, hence, the production of smaller mechanical toys.

Some of the earliest of these, among them a small coach worked by clockwork and a galley which could be rowed mechanically, were made by a toymaker named Heroard, and given to Louis XIII in 1608, when he was seven years old and still Dauphin of France. Two other examples of this high quality German craftsmanship encouraged by royal patronage are the set of performing silver toy soldiers, made in 1672 for a child of Louis XIV by two Nuremberg craftsmen named Hautsch, and a mechanical carousel, 'The Little World', picturing men at work in a variety of trades, which Gottfried Hautsch made for the Bavarian Court in 1702. Thereafter and throughout the whole of the eighteenth century, when royal patronage was no longer crucial, and when mechanical toys and automata began to be made for a somewhat wider market, the French and Swiss became the leaders of an industry that was to see toys begin to be mass-produced throughout the world. The real history, thus, really begins in the eighteenth century.

Suddenly, the mechanical toy ceased to be a plaything merely for the privileged, and, in a wide variety of forms, became a commonplace possession of almost every middle-class child. Since then, toy trains, ships, cars, and comic figures have been driven over acres of nursery floor by successive generations of children; dolls, activated by a variety of machinery enabling them to do almost anything from crying to walking, talking, or singing, have been forced unremittingly to perform by many a strong-minded owner; mechanical banks have encouraged the virtues of saving; toy pianos, polyphons, and musical boxes, the pleasures of music. There is now virtually nothing that cannot be made on a miniature scale, and, broadly speaking, with a wider sector of the population now able and willing to indulge and educate their young, the incentive for the toymaker or manufacturer is greater than ever before.

The Age of the Craftsman

In eighteenth-century Europe, the aristocratic and royal tone of society became modified by the greater power and wealth of the commercial and professional classes. Science had finally come into its own with the establishment of scientific academies at the end of the seventeenth century in France, England and Italy; and with the continuation of the great open fairs and competitions, the public developed a thirst for mechanical novelties, whether they were regarded as toys for children or as adult amusements – a distinction which was difficult to maintain at the time. The Tuileries Palace and St. Germain were two of the places where showmen could perform and inventors and toymakers could display their wares, and which helped to develop the reputations of such outstanding craftsmen as Jacques de Vaucanson and Pierre Jaquet-Droz.

De Vaucanson, who was born in Grenoble in 1709, and who was said to have studied mechanics in Paris, became internationally famous for his ingenious and intricate automata. One of these, exhibited at St. Germain in 1749, was a grocer with a little shop who filled the orders given to him by audiences at the fairs, but the piece that seems to have been the most ingenious was a life-sized gilded mechanical duck.

Life-sized mechanical flute player, duck, and tambourine player made by Jacques de Vaucanson. 1738.

Described as being anatomically exact in the structure and movement of its bones and the placing of its (rubber) intestines, it quacked, moved its head and wings, stretched out its neck to gobble up grain, digested by means of a chemical solvent, and convincingly disposed of waste in the normal way. De Vaucanson's duck passed through several hands after he gave up showmanship for a more conventional scientific career, and was still regarded as a marvel in the mid-nineteenth century, but it eventually disappeared, as did the master's other works.

Jaquet-Droz, a younger contemporary of de Vaucanson, is widely regarded as the master

Life-sized mechanical silver swan by James Cox. It was once housed on an enormous stand with mirrors that produced multiple reflections and stood on a bejewelled base. Above the swan was a dome crowned by a rising sun with rays which radiated from it. The whole construction was nearly 5.4 m (18 ft) high. The swan, which has an articulated neck and moveable bill, begins its action by preening, and then bends towards the 'water' and appears to pick up one of the silver fish, which are mounted on the rotating glass rods in front of the swan. Finally, the swan appears to swallow the fish as it raises its neck, but, actually, the fish swallowed is one already concealed within the swan's beak. It is probable that Cox imported the highly complicated mechanism of the neck in the mid-18th century and then developed the more conventional movements himself. Bowes Museum, Barnard Castle.

among masters. He was born in 1721 at La Chaux de Fonds, Switzerland, and was intended for the Church until he revealed a quite exceptional aptitude for watchmaking. Like many craftsmen who made automata and luxury toys, Jaquet-Droz developed his skills in this traditional Swiss industry. His first great success was with a tiny mechanical singing bird fitted into a snuff box, which seemed to have been the first of its kind. This and his watches and clocks with automata, led to his being invited to the Spanish Court (1758–9), where he might have been usefully subsidized had the religious fanatics not been suspicious of his works, and his visit not been curtailed by the king's death. It is probable that he began work shortly afterwards on the life-sized mechanical figures for which he is now chiefly remembered: the Artist, the Writer and the Musician (discussed in Chapter

Seven), all of which are still in working order and can now be seen at the Musée d'Art et d'Histoire in Neuchâtel. All look surprisingly real and have eyes that move, worked from within their beautifully sculptured heads.

Both the Artist and the Writer were presented as curly-headed small boys. The Artist had a repertoire of four different pictures, including George III and Queen Charlotte of England, and Marie Antoinette and Louis XVI of France. By means of a bellows mechanism in his head, the Artist could also blow the drying powder from his paper as he paused between drawings. The Writer is still more impressive in its realism and mechanical complexity. He sits on a stool, holding his quill pen ready, and when set in motion, he dips the pen in the inkwell in front of him, shakes it, and then writes, his eyes regularly glancing at the sheet of paper he is supposed to be

The Writer, an automaton made by Pierre Jaquet-Droz. Musée d'Art et d'Histoire, Neuchâtel.

on his past record it is reasonable to assume that Pierre Jaquet-Droz's was the master hand. Both Henri-Louis and Leschot helped to exhibit Jaquet-Droz's figures around Europe. In 1774, the year the figures were presented to the public for the first time, Henri-Louis visited Paris with the Artist and was ordered to give a command performance before Marie Antoinette and Louis XVI. The royal couple were apparently fascinated by the automaton and made him perform for them again and again. Later still, Henri-Louis, who became a master in his own right, brought the Artist to England, where he set up a branch of the firm and demonstrated the automaton to George III and Queen Charlotte, having it draw their pictures.

Henri Maillardet is another Swiss, who like Leschot, started his career as Pierre Jaquet-Droz's apprentice and who, like Henri-Louis, became a master craftsman and exhibited his work in London. Unluckily for his reputation, the only item to survive is a version he made of the Writer. It differs from Jaquet-Droz's original in several respects, especially in its complicated curlicued design, and is now in the Franklin Institute, Philadelphia, where it has been re-dressed as a girl. Henri's brother, Jean David Maillardet, who was eventually assisted by his sons, was responsible for a number of automata, among them a clock with a dunce's-capped magician who tells fortunes by pointing to a panel in which predictions appear. This piece still exists and can be seen at the Musée d'Horologie at La Chaux de Fonds.

Some English craftsmen of considerable note were also working at this time. Christopher Pinchbeck, chiefly remembered as the inventor of a zinc-and-copper alloy that can pass for gold (whence Pinchbeck) was also a watchmaker; an organ builder; possibly the first man to discover the musical box movement; and,

copying. He can be pre-set to write a message of two or three sentences, leaving the correct spaces between words and starting a fresh line at regular intervals. Both the Artist and the Writer were worked by means of changeable sets of cams that were mounted on a cylinder turned by clockwork.

Jaquet-Droz was helped by his son Henri-Louis and by his assistant, Jean Frederic Leschot, who was also an exceptionally gifted craftsman. It is now impossible to say who was chiefly responsible for these figures; but if his advertisements are to be believed, a maker of mechanical figures in the 1720's, before de Vaucanson came on the European scene.

A more spectacular figure was James Cox, a jeweller from Shoe Lane, London, who held an exhibition in 1772 in the Spring Gardens, near Whitehall, which understandably caused a sensation. Cox's assemblage of fifty-six mechanical animals and birds and scenes on clocks must have constituted the greatest collection of automata ever put on show for the benefit of the public, but, unfortunately, Cox charged half a guinea a head – enough to pay an agricultural labourer for a long week's work – and thus attracted a clientele so select he could not afford to keep the exhibition going. Instead, he put its contents up as prizes in a lottery, with the result that they were scattered and have largely disappeared. However, the *pièce de résistance*, a silver swan that appears to catch and swallow a fish, and swims on a surface over which rotating crystal rods create an illusion of watery motion, has survived and forms part of the collection of the Bowes Museum near Barnard Castle, County Durham. Cox also made a good many luxury items for princely customers in the East who were even more avid for expensive wonders than the monarchs of Europe. One such piece, which must have been made in the Orient in the eighteenth century, is Tippoo's Tiger. It once belonged to Tipu Sultan, ruler of Mysore, and is now in the Victoria and Albert Museum, London. This life-sized (1.778 m. (5.86 ft) long) statue of a wooden tiger mauling a European (whose left arm is raised in a feeble effort to fence the beast off), contains an organ that, when its handle is turned, produces a tigerish snarling and harrowing human screams. There is a strong likelihood that Tippoo's Tiger was inspired by the accidental death of a British General's son,

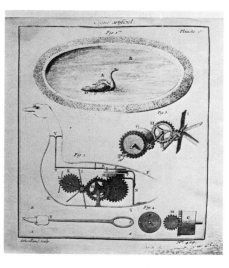

and that the anti-British Tipu enjoyed watching the re-enactment of the tragedy. The poet John Keats must have heard the story and seen Tippoo's Tiger at the East India Museum in London, where it was taken after the defeat and death of Tipu at the battle of Seringapatam in 1799. In the mock-heroic *The Cap and Bells, and Plaything of the Emperor's Choice,* Keats transformed India into a Fairy City with a Tipu-like ruler, Emperor Elfinian, whose page had less fear of:

A dose of senna-tea or nightmare Gorgon Than the Emperor when he played on his Man-Tiger Organ.

Automata was a particularly acceptable form of tribute since western science and technology

had outstripped that of China. European visitors, from the Jesuits to the eighteenth-century ambassadors from the west, brought clocks, mechanical animals, musical boxes and similar items. Often these were made of precious metals and studded with jewels. The Peking Museum still has an English clock with a forty-centimetre-high writing figure made by Pierre Jaquet-Droz. It is dressed in eighteenth-century European fashion but has acquired, possibly through re-painting, somewhat Orientalised features and writes a short message in Chinese characters.

The stimulus of this trade to western craftsmanship must have been considerable, in particular with regard to encouraging the

17

VOITURE EN CARTON A MOUVEMENT D'HORLOGERIE
VOITURE MÉCANIQUE EN MÉTAL ORNÉE DE PERSONNAGES EN VERRERIE DE NEVERS
XVIIIᵉ SIÈCLE. — (COLLECTION DE M. HENRY D'ALLEMAGNE)

Carriage with clockwork movement, and mechanical carriage. 18th cent. From *Histoire des Jouets* by Henri d'Allemagne.

development of miniature workmanship, but it is difficult to ascertain the extent to which technical advances were preserved and handed on. In the eighteenth century the mechanical and the marvellous were still closely related; indeed, in spite of vigorous attempts to spread scientific knowledge, a near-superstitious attitude towards mechanical and optical devices persisted well into the Victorian period. De Vaucanson, it is said, ended his first career of Jesuit seminarist after making some flying angels – an achievement which his teachers evidently regarded as diabolically inspired; and the Inquisition is supposed to have investigated Jaquet-Droz during his stay in Spain. The confusion of the public is all the more understandable if one takes into account its naïvety at this early stage in the history of technology, and the fact that the makers of automata concealed their methods as jealously as magicians guard their professional secrets. Indeed, technology and magic were deliberately confused by some individuals who put on displays that combined elements of both.

One example of this was The Automaton Chess Player, otherwise called The Turk, which was – or was claimed to be – the first chess-playing machine. The Turk, a turbaned and moustachioed life-sized figure, sat in front of a large cabinet topped with a chess board and chess set. Before a game began, the doors of the cabinet were flung open to reveal machinery, and nothing but machinery. The Turk played, accompanied by impressive whirrings and clankings, always moving the pieces with his left hand. Made by Baron Wolfgang von Kempelen, who was certainly an inventor of genuine ability, the Turk appeared at the Austrian court in 1780, and for the next seventy years was exhibited at various fairs and took on all players including Napoleon, who lost. On von Kempelen's death, the Turk was taken over by Johann Nepomuk Maelzel, who was notable for perfecting the metronome and devising a number of ingenious automata such as the panharmonicon, a complete orchestra for which his friend Beethoven composed the 'Battle Symphony'. Maelzel took the Turk to the United States in 1826, and some years later both he and its operator were carried off by Yellow Fever, and the Turk ended his days, with singular inappropriateness, in the Chinese Museum in Philadelphia, which was destroyed by fire in 1854. The secret of the Turk died with him, but no one seriously doubts that a human operator was hidden somewhere inside him. Most writers are inclined to believe that the chess pieces were magnetised, and that corresponding magnetic discs under the board but inside the cabinet enabled the operator to keep track of what was happening. Whatever the truth may be, it should be pointed out that the Turk was a fake only in the terms of the claims made for it. It must have been a formidable piece of machinery by the standards of the age.

The same can be said of its successors. Mephisto, exhibited from 1878, even entered and won an English tournament, and was secretly operated for a time by a still more famous player, Harry Nelson Pillsbury (like most professional chess players in those days, he was poverty-stricken). It was eventually relegated to Coney Island where it too was destroyed by fire. The taste for this kind of entertainment was not confined to chess players: for well over a quarter of a century, down to 1910, the showman Neville John Maskelyne demonstrated an automaton named Psycho that could play cards with members of its London audience, as well as perform smoking and other tricks. Like other pseudo-automata, Psycho looked like a refugee from some imaginary eastern country, with dark skin, a plumed hat and wildly patterned silk tunic. We are less romantic about our machines nowadays, even when they work without covert assistance. Over the last few years the chess machine has once again come to the fore – the computer. In the age of the silicone chip, which has seen computers miniaturised to become pocket calculators, it must be only a

matter of time before fanatics of all ages can play against a pocket electronic opponent.

Another of the successful nineteenth-century showmen who exhibited automata was a Frenchman named Eugène Robert-Houdin. Although little remembered today, he was the most famous magician of the nineteenth century – so famous in fact that years after his death, the American escapologist Ehrich

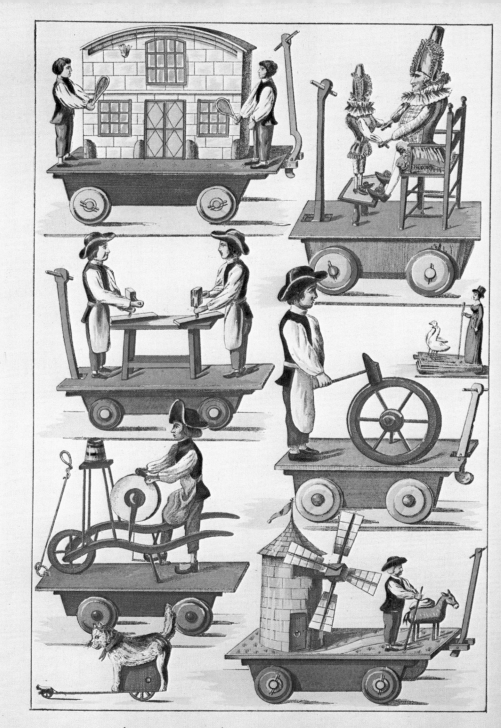

JOUETS MÉCANIQUES REPRÉSENTANT DIVERS JEUX ET PROFESSIONS
(MODÈLES TIRÉS DE L'ALBUM D'UN FABRICANT DE JOUETS)
ÉPOQUE EMPIRE

Mechanical toys depicting different games and professions. Taken from a toy manufacturer's catalogue of the Empire period by Henri d'Allemagne for his *Histoire des Jouets.*

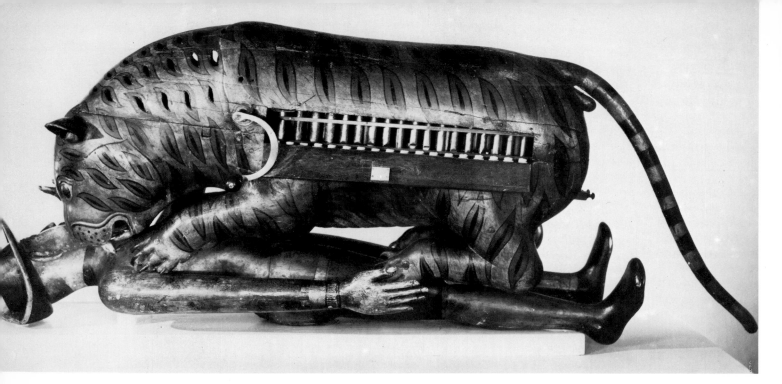

THE AUTOMATON CHESS PLAYER.

Top
Tipoo's Tiger. Made for the amusement of Tipu, Sultan of Mysore. *c.* 1790. Length: 1.778 m (5.86 ft). Victoria and Albert Museum, London.

Above
The Turk, an automaton chess player made by a Hungarian, Baron Wolfgang von Kempelen. From an early 19th cent. engraving.

Weiss thought Robert-Houdin's name still had sufficient publicity value to make it worth his while calling himself Houdini. The climax of Robert-Houdin's career occurred in the 1840s, when he gave a number of demonstrations at the Palais Royale in Paris, followed by a tour all over England. Among the automata involved in the shows were a little writer roughly similar to Jaquet-Droz's and a musketeer that fired at a target. Robert-Houdin had

been a clockmaker's apprentice and himself may have made some or all of the automata which, unlike von Kempelen's, seem to have been basically honest. On the other hand, there was certainly an element of illusionism involved, but to what extent it is now impossible to say since both the automata and Robert-Houdin's records were destroyed in the 1920s, before any competent investigator had made a proper study of them. Like other magicians, Robert-Houdin was quite ready to boast of his feats in print, but not to explain them.

Although only luxury items have been discussed so far, fairly cheap mechanical toys were available in the late eighteenth and early nineteenth centuries, among the earliest being those made by French prisoners in England during the long Napoleonic Wars. At Norman Cross, near Peterborough, seven thousand French prisoners (some of them who spent ten years or more in captivity) passed the time by whittling away at bones or pieces of wood, shaping and fitting them together to construct ingenious model buildings, soldiers, ships and games which they then sold to the local people. The best-known of these makers was a sailor named Père Cruchet, who was captured after the battle of Trafalgar in 1805. He is credited with devising fine lever-operated toys, as well as clockwork versions which were much more economically constructed than earlier toys of that type. However, his precise contribution is difficult to determine, as is his actual influence on later English and French toys. What does seem to be established is that he introduced the English to a working toy version of the *guillotine*, at that time held in especial horror because of its deployment during the Terror in the French Revolutionary period.

There is good evidence that before 1850 cheap mechanical toys were being made in London, and even cheaper ones in France and Germany. Henry Mayhew, whose *London Life and the London Poor* is one of the earliest classics of sociological investigation, gives a grim picture of the English toymaker's struggle to survive, as does this statement by an English importer, quoted in an 1850 *Morning Chronicle*:

Few watchmakers here can repair a clockwork mouse; they will generally charge 2s 6d for repairing a mechanical mouse (imported from France) which I sell new for 3s 6d. Such a mouse could not be made here if it could be made at all for less than 15s.

In this instance, the toymaker's difficulties had been accentuated by the lowering of protective tariffs on toys which was part of Sir Robert Peel's Free Trade measures of the 1840s. However, there were plenty of poor and exploited toymakers before that, as Charles Dickens noted in his Christmas Story *The Cricket on the Hearth* (published in 1845 but quite possibly reflecting conditions some years earlier). Dicken's Caleb Plummer is, 'a little, meagre, thoughtful, dingy-faced man, who seemed to have made himself a great-coat from the sack-cloth covering of some old box'; who lived in 'a little cracked nutshell of a wooden house' with cracked ceilings, mouldering beams and peeling wallpaper and who strove for authenticity as much as his real-life counterparts:

Below Left
Psycho, an automaton card player made by Neville John Maskelyne. Museum of London.

Below Right
Rear view of Maskelyne's Psycho. Museum of London.

" You couldn't have the goodness to let me pinch Boxer's tail, Mum, for half a moment, could you ?"
" Why, Caleb! What a question!"
" Oh never mind, Mum," said the little man. "He mightn't like it perhaps. There's a small order just come in, for barking dogs; and I should wish to go as close to Natur' as I could, for sixpence. That's all. Never mind, Mum."

Dickens gives a graphic description of the poor toymaker's workshop and its contents, the majority of which, apart from dolls, dolls' houses and Noah's Arks, were mechanical:

There were scores of melancholy little carts which, when the wheels went round, performed most doleful music. Many small fiddles, drums, and other instruments of torture; no end of cannon, shields, swords, spears, and guns. There were little tumblers in red breeches, incessantly swarming up high obstacles of red-tape, and coming down, head first, on the other side; and there were innumerable old gentlemen of respectable, not to say venerable, appearance, insanely flying over horizontal pegs, inserted, for the purpose, in their own street doors. There were beasts of all sorts; horses in particular ... it would have been hard to count the dozens upon dozens of grotesque figures that were ever ready to commit all sorts of absurdities on the turning of a handle ...

At least some of this represents Dickens's childhood memories; elsewhere he recalls his music-cart, and 'the little tumbler in his shirt sleeves, perpetually swarming up one side of a wooden frame, and coming down, head foremost, on the other', whom he thought even then 'rather a weak-minded person'. These items therefore date back to about 1820, and were cheap enough for Dickens's Micawber-like father to be able to afford.

In the nineteenth century, Britain was at the heart of new developments, and by mid-century was becoming known as the 'Workshop of the World'. The Great Exhibition of 1851 was planned as a sort of British apotheosis – a mammoth display of the arts and industries of all nations, in which Britain would inevitably take the leading place. Held at the Crystal Palace, especially erected over nineteen acres of Hyde Park to house the exhibition, it marked a step forward in scope and organisation from the fairs and exhibitions of the eighteenth century. According to the Exhibition's *Official Descriptive and Illustrative Catalogue*, mechanical toys made a respectable showing, those from Austria and Germany (from Bavaria, the Tyrol, Vienna, and Bohemia – whose craftwork was

Above
The Crystal Palace, location of the Great Exhibition, 1851. Lithograph by Vincent Brooks.

Right
Clockwork automaton of fur rabbit violinist with painted wooden paws and violin. Height: 50.8 cm (20 in). Christie's, London.

still famous) being the most prominent. But not all of the German toys were of the expected sort: those from Württemberg, which the catalogue confirmed were exported to various countries and were known throughout Europe and America, included tableaux of frogs being shaved and cats dancing – not wooden or metal toys, but stuffed real animals.

The most exciting catalogue entry was that of A. Bouchet of 74 Baker Street, London:

Animated and musical tableau, representing the Great Exhibition and peoples of all Nations. Panoptic polyrama. Evening games. Knight in armour, complete with horse caparisoned. Animal trophies and saracen armour. Balloon. Various mechanical toys. Dolls and shops.

E. C. Spurin of New Bond Street was represented by another ambitious item: 'Mechanical toy model of an English farm with figures, threshing machine, windmill, etc., in action.' Another entry, by E. and Clara Bursill of

P. 23

The object . . . was to buy up all the prettier toys that were yet to be met with, it being very clear to me that there would soon occur a break in my regular consignments from the French capital; and the probability stared me in the face of our little ones at home sickening of ennui for the want of their old favourite toys, after they should have exhausted the strength of both the out and the indoor patients of Dolly's Hospital.

Hornsey Road, was worded with true British reserve: 'Compressible toys'. Presumably, it meant toys worked on the bellows principle – for example, with a concertina base, so that when the toy was pushed down and then released, figures were moved or noises emitted by air pressure.

Another glimpse of the toymaking of that age is given by Henry Cremer whose toy-shop in Regent Street was one of the most important in London. Though evidently a successful businessman who personally visited France and Germany as a buyer, Cremer, in his *Toys of the Little Folk of All Ages and Countries* (1873) wrote about toys and children with extreme sentimentality exemplified in this entry of August 1870, when Cremer visited Paris which at that time was about to be beseiged by Prussian troops:

Cremer visited a gunmaker, a sword manufacturer, maker of accessories for dolls and of grotesque 'surprise' toys, but without much luck, since most of the businesses were turned over to war production or were short-staffed, their employees having been called to the front. In response to this situation, Cremer remarked that,

we cannot get on, you know, without French toys, for the gaieté de coeur *of the nursery depends very much upon a continuous supply of these ingenious and mirth-producing contrivances.*

However, he managed to buy a large number of toy guns, 'leaving

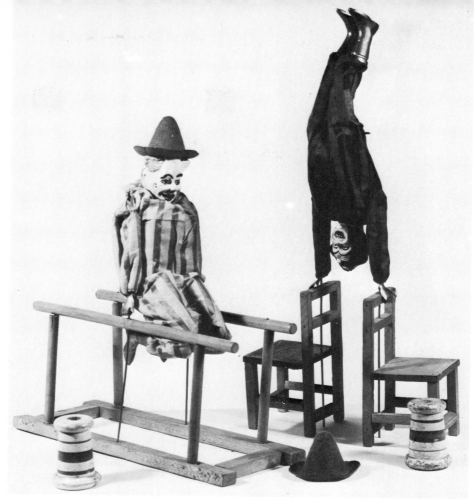

very little for any requisitions which might be made by the advancing forces.' On the other hand, Cremer added:

It was utterly impossible to get anything done that required clockwork; and it was not reasonable to expect that men could sit themselves down to adjust the minute details of toy machinery whilst the thought of war engrossed their minds. So I turned my attention to the animal kingdom . . . I left very little or no toy mutton, horse, donkey, or dog, in Paris. I requisitioned all the properties of sheep, horses, asses and the canine species I could find; and the Parisians must by this time have almost forgotten the sound of the bleating of sheep, the neighing of horses, the braying of asses, and the barking of dogs – in the toy world.

And, one might add, in the real world: shortly after Cremer's requisitioning, the Prussians besieged Paris and the starving inhabitants were reduced to eating rats and cats.

Whatever its shortcomings, Cremer's account does indicate the importance of the French toy industry in 1870. This was also claimed earlier by another English importer who told the

Morning Chronicle that:

None in my opinion can be compared to the French in the ingenuity of their toys – they surpass the skill of the best English workmen.

But, it was for luxury toys primarily that France was to remain pre-eminent. By Cremer's time, cheaper versions of French toys – clockwork and otherwise – were already being produced in quantities by German manufacturers. The effects of German competition were probably felt all the more quickly because of France's defeat in 1870, which disrupted her production and must have persuaded established customers like Cremer to look elsewhere for their supplies:

Dolly's horse had gone up in the French market [up in price], and I therefore resolved to see what could be done for her in this respect in another emporium.

A year later, at the London International Exhibition, German toys were already out in force – at a vastly more competitive price.

The Dawn of Mass-Production

There was a certain justice in the fact that Germany pioneered the mass-production of mechanical toys. Her toymaking tradition was the oldest in Europe: even in the fifteenth century the Nuremberg-Fürth area was exporting toys in such quantities that a commissioner was appointed to co-ordinate and control the various makers. By the nineteenth century, toy centres included not only Nuremberg, but also Sonneberg in Thuringia, famous for dolls, and the Black Forest and Saxony, which mainly produced wooden toys. After the Prussian defeat of France and the economic and political unification of Germany – previously divided into many separate states – culminating in the foundation of the German Empire, Germany emerged as one of the major industrial powers, overtaking France and rivalling Britain.

Ultimately, German superiority did not depend on a single technological advance, but rather on a combination of accumulated skills, initiative and hard work, aided by governmental subsidies of transport and other concessions. But one advance that the German firms did benefit from was a process, invented in France in 1815, by which power presses stamped out dozens of parts from a single sheet of tin plate (thin metal with a coating of tin). This enabled firms to produce very cheap mechanical toys in quantity.

The manufacture of tin plate provides an early example of recycling in France and Germany, at least, where poor people could earn a little money by collecting food cans and other discarded items made of tin. These were melted down for re-use by toymakers, and the metal was then made into sheets and painted in bold gleaming colours before it was stamped out. Broad effects could be achieved by dipping or spraying, but details had to be hand-painted, stencilled, or put on by transfer printing until the 1890s, when offset

Above
Bagatelle player. German.
c. 1900-14. Private collection.

Opposite Top
Lithographed penny toys with simple mechanisms by different makers. Private collection.

Opposite Bottom
Clock with an automaton magician; made in the Black Forest region of Germany. 1850. Height: 58 cm (23 in). Abeler Museum, Wuppertal.

lithography was introduced, making production far quicker and cheaper.

Two other advances that helped speed up production were the manufacture of cheaper and less elaborate clockwork movements, and the development of the friction-drive mechanism.

The basic friction-drive mechanism consisted of a heavy flywheel centred on the axle attached to the wheels of the toy. The toy was set in motion by rotating the flywheel sharply (on the palm of the hand or along the ground), or, in some instances, by tugging a string or toothed bar. The flywheel then turned the axle (and therefore the toy's wheels) until it ran out of momentum.

Friction-driven toys were popular in the late nineteenth century, but clockwork remained the most common device for making toys move. However, both systems were used to drive the cheap mass-produced tinplate 'penny toy', the simplest of which consisted of two parts meeting

around the drive mechanism. These parts, stamped out shallowly and giving the ensuing figure an appearance somewhere between profile and three-dimensionality, were not usually soldered, but stapled together by the tongue and slot method which, with care, gave excellent (invisible-join) results. The whole range of toys, including the more expensive ones, sometimes comprising dozens of parts, were ingenious, whimsical, sometimes grotesque or slightly sentimental, and all extraordinarily appealing to the world-wide markets which received them with open arms and brought fame to their German manufacturers.

Nuremberg, with its metalworking and toymaking tradition, was the natural centre for producing this type of clockwork tinplate toy and similar items, and most of the great firms of the 'golden age' until 1914 – and the 'iron age' after it – operated in the area. It also became a manufacturing centre for toys operated by steam.

The railway museum and 'steam fairs' are capable of attracting large numbers now, in the electronic age, but in the nineteenth century, with factories and workshops thundering and railway networks criss-crossing over the land, steam was strange, new, and magical, and children and adults alike were fascinated by the steam engine and its noisy, dirty, and spectacular harnessing of power.

Early examples of miniature steam-driven engines occupy the debatable territory between models and toys, but after 1870 large numbers were marketed and advertised in magazines and catalogues as suitable for children. Of course, it is likely that the 'steam set', like later clockwork and electric train sets, was used as often by parents as by their children. Their collaboration must have been quite usual since operating the intimidating mass of boilers, cylinders, pipes, rods and wheels that made up the steam engine was much more complicated than any previously manufactured toy. There was plenty to do: the boiler had to be filled with water, the fire started (in toy terms: a spirit burner lit and placed under the boiler), the steam turned on, and everything frequently checked and lubricated.

Some of the engines were produced for purely spectacular reasons with parts made of glass enabling observation of the engine's workings, but most of them were made for more functional purposes: to drive a miniature distillery, windmill, fountain, printing press, circus roundabout, or Great Wheel. Although cheap rudimentary engines were by no means unknown, many were strong and accurately reproduced, with gleaming polished parts, the machinery they drove capable of being equally impressive. Steam was also used, though less realistically, to move a variety of human figures, who sawed, ground knives, turned wheels, or even laboured collectively on the assembly line. For added realism, firms like the Union Manufacturing Company of Brooklyn, New York, sold a whole range of machine tools and similar steam-driven accessories, but the most exciting of all steam-driven toys were of course the various types of transport: the fire engine, with its brilliant red bodywork and exposed copper working parts; the steam-roller; some superb boats, including convincing working copies of gunboats; and from the 1890s, even some early automobiles.

Above all, there were locomotives – the very embodiment of the Age of Steam. They were the most popular of all steam toys, and for years the really dedicated railway buff believed that people who played with clockwork were members of an inferior species: only steam was authentic, and only steam made the miniature locomotive move, clank and hiss (though not, alas, roar) like the real thing. The market was large enough to

absorb all sorts of versions, from the cheapest and shoddiest tinplate to the most glamorous and aggressive scale-models.

Gebrüder Bing (Bing Brothers) was the leading Nuremberg maker of steam-driven toys and for a time in the 1880s it led the world. It developed from the wholesale business run by Ignaz and Adolf Bing in the 1860s, first making metal toys and then scale-model locomotives as well as optical and kinetic toys. Like many other firms, Bing collapsed in the Great Depression and was

taken over in 1933 by a lesser known rival, Karl Bub.

History dealt just as badly with Georges Carette, a Frenchman, who set up a toy firm in Nuremberg in 1886 – a time when businessmen tended to be fairly internationally-minded despite the political uncertainties – selling soldiers, weapons, gunboats, and military vehicles quite impartially to anyone who would buy, obligingly changing the German flag for the Union Jack or the *Bismark* for the *Gambetta*. Carette built up a flourishing business in

electric and clockwork toys, and also took part in the development of scale-model locomotives. But the First World War made it impossible for him to remain in Germany, and the Carette firm disappeared in 1917.

Other firms established in Nuremberg before 1900 included such well-known names as Hess, Günthermann, Fleischmann, Planck, and Meier, and a good many more were established in the early years of the twentieth century. Zirndorf, a village just outside Nuremberg where Mangold and other manufacturers set up, was another centre, as was nearby Fürth, virtually Nuremberg's twin city, which was linked up to Nuremberg by an eight-kilometre (4.8 mi) railway line – the first to be laid in Germany – which indicates the economic importance of toymaking in the nineteenth century.

A few other toy manufacturers set up in the Stuttgart area, some 150 kilometres (90 mi) south-west of Nuremberg. Easily the most important of these was Märklin at Göppingen. The business originated in 1859 with Theodor Märklin, a tinsmith who added toy kitchenware and wheeled toys to his normal range of wares. Soon he was in charge of his own factory. His wife, Karoline, seems

Above
Early spirit-painted and lithographed penny toys. The paddle steamer was made by Gebrüder Bing of Nuremberg *c.* 1902. The large engine in the middle which carries the initials PLM (Paris-Lyon-Marseilles) is probably German-made. Private collection.

Right
Clockwork toy. German. Early 20th cent. Bethnal Green Museum, London.

Opposite
Clockwork trains. *c.* 1840. Bethnal Green Museum, London.

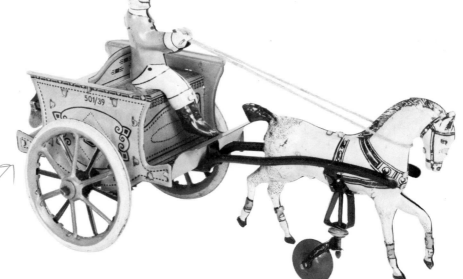

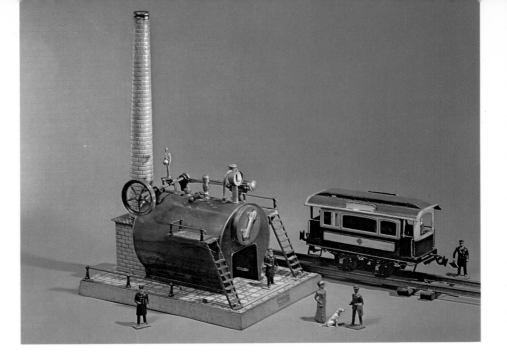

Right
Bing steam engine, *c.* 1902; and
Carette hand-painted Guage '1' street
car, *c.* 1904, which has an electric
mechanism that runs off a wet-cell
battery. Private collection.

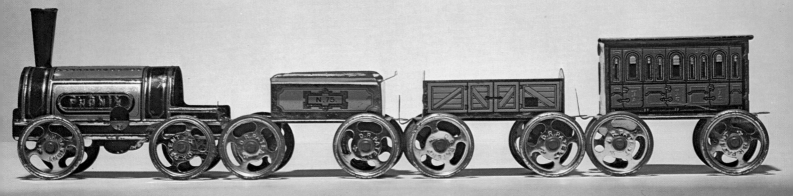

Above
Transfer-printed train by Hess of
Nuremberg which could also be
operated by a flywheel. Most
manufacturers made toys at a variety
of prices and with or without
mechanisms. Private collection.

to have been the driving force
behind the enterprise, travelling
through South Germany and
Switzerland in search of orders,
but when Theodor died in 1866,
the business fell on hard times and
came to a standstill. It was
revived only in the 1880s, when
Theodor's three sons, Eugen,
Wilhelm and Karl, combined
their managerial and technical
skills and started what was to
become the famous Märklin
Brothers (Gebrüder Märklin)
firm, which is still in existence.

The Märklins' distinctive
contribution was to initiate the
movement towards realism in
locomotive and railway making.
German makers had sold
clockwork locomotives running
on rails from some time in the
1860s, but the Märklins made the
first railways with crossings,
switches and points, and figure-
eight layouts; these were a

tremendous success at the Leipzig
Spring Fair of 1891, and brought
the firm the backing it needed to
mass-produce steam and
electrically driven scale-models.
Bing and others followed suit, and
the scale-model railway industry
was born.

Scale-models are rather
different from ordinary toys. In
fact most model enthusiasts would
indignantly reject the idea that
their hobby had anything at all to
do with toys, and there is certainly
a point beyond which it can no
longer be considered child's play,
in any sense of the term. The
'ordinary' toy train (or boat or car
or plane) is not a failed copy but it
simplifies reality, omitting
irrelevant detail and emphasising
crucial elements such as boilers
and funnels.

Great German firms like
Märklin, Bing and Planck had a
large export business in toy steam

locomotives, creating and appropriately labelling a range of British and French types, and even selling versions of the 'cow-catcher' locomotive in its native United States. In England, the scale-modelling movement was started by Wenman Bassett-Lowke, who was able to use the facilities at his father's Northampton engineering factory. Besides being a good businessman, he was a fanatical perfectionist and a scale-model enthusiast. Inspired by the German locomotives he saw at the 1900 Paris Exhibition, Bassett-Lowke aimed for a still greater precision, which he achieved by working in collaboration with the engineer Henry Greenly, who joined the firm as technical advisor. Bassett-Lowke quickly established close relationships with Bing, Carette and other German firms, with the result that

the various components of a particular model were often manufactured by two or three different firms. This international co-operation was brought to an end by the First World War, but was resumed surprisingly quickly once hostilities had ended. Ideas were exchanged as well, and, in a sense, Bassett-Lowke could be said to have kept the Germans' standards up, since only in collaboration with him did they produce true models rather than high quality toys, but, ultimately, they lacked Bassett-Lowke's passion for accuracy in all things.

In terms of mechanical toys, American history begins in the nineteenth century, its early makers developing from metalworking or clockmaking backgrounds. George W. Brown, for example, had been apprenticed to a clockmaker before setting up a business with

Friction-driven cars made by Hess between 1900-14. The crank turns a heavy flywheel which then drives the front wheels. The start/stop mechanism is controlled by turning the steering wheel. The 1913 Gamage's catalogue describes the green car as a hill climbing car. Private collection.

another clockmaker named Chauncey Goodrich in 1856 in Forestville, now part of Bristol, Connecticut – long the primary toymaking state in the Union. From clocks they went on to produce a wide range of tin toys. As well as the familiar range of riders, vehicles, and boats, Brown devised a circus wagon containing a clockwork lion that paced up and down as the wagon moved; a machine shop; and a doll pushing a double hoop with a Liberty Bell at the front and a boy standing on the axle carrying the Stars and Stripes. Similar hoop toys were also manufactured by Althof,

Bergmann & Co. in the 1870s. For a few years (1868–72), Brown's tin-toy firm merged with J. & E. Stevens, who were iron-toy manufacturers, but Brown seems to have dropped out of the toymaking industry altogether at the end of the 1870s.

The most notable American toymaker was Edward Riley Ives, who seems to have started by helping his farmer father make hot-air toys (which were very popular in nineteenth-century America) as a sideline. In 1870, Ives left his home in the small town of Plymouth, Connecticut – within easy walking distance of

Right
Clown Artist, made by Philip Vielmetter of Germany, c. 1900, which works on the same principle as Pierre Jaquet-Droz's Artist automaton: different sets of cams incorporated in the clown's base enable it to draw a variety of pictures, including Queen Victoria and the Czarina. Private collection.

Below
Steam engine and sawyers made by Ernst Planck. 1895. Base: 27.3 cm (10.9 in) long. Jacques Milet collection.

Forestville – and set up a toy factory at the larger and better-sited coastal city of Bridgeport, about fifty kilometres further south. This factory was to become world famous, first under Ives and later under his son Harry C. Ives, but it was closed in 1929 due to the pressures caused by the Great Depression.

Ives was an inventive man and patented some toys in his own name, but, like other great manufacturers, he had the gift of attracting other inventors who either worked directly for him or sold him their ideas (apparently Ives was wisely generous in his royalty arrangements). One of the earliest of all Ives's mechanical toys – an oarsman who could actually row his little boat on the water – was patented by Nathan S. Warner, but perhaps the most talented of the inventors was Jerome B. Secor, who had specialised in machine tools but joined up with Ives after living next to him for a while at Bridgeport. Secor devised a gun, a locomotive, a singing bird, and various other musical toys.

In the 1880s, Ives expanded steadily, taking over the Automatic Toy Works in New York, although Bridgeport continued to be the firm's 'main office'. At about the same time, Ives began manufacturing iron toys, and a few years later, the Hubley Company of Lancaster, Pennsylvania, also entered the field. In the early years of the twentieth century there were even American cast-iron toy automobiles of a rather rudimentary kind. However, the best iron toys were those made by the J. & E. Stevens Company.

Top
Märklin spirit-fired portable steam engine with brass boiler. Length: 26 cm (10.25 in). Sotheby's, London.

Above
Ernst Planck Gauge '3' steam train set with original box. c. 1905. Length of coach: 13 cm (5.25 in). Sotheby's, London.

Ives showed a characteristically nineteenth-century American interest in the events and personalities of the day, and made toy representations of women's rights agitators and a smoking man modelled to represent Ulysses S. Grant. Like other Americans, Ives was also particularly alive to the romance of the railroad, since this was its epic age in the United States. The Union Pacific Co. completed the first coast-to-coast transcontinental railway in 1869, and over the next few decades, the railroad, at least as much as any other force, reached out over the land and tamed it, as did the American toy manufacturers who became active producers of steam-

driven locomotives from the 1870s on: Ives and Buckman; the Eugene Begs Co. of Paterson, New Jersey; and from the 1880s on, the Weedon Manufacturing Company of New Bedford, which became the leader of the American market and survived long after most of its rivals had succumbed to competition from clockwork and electricity.

The popularity of steam toys in the last years of the century can be gauged from the catalogues. The Montgomery Ward company advertised Weeden steam trains and boats to run 'in a tub or tank of water or on a still water pond', and also boasted a New Steam Fire Engine, featuring two cylinders; pump and hose

Above
Front: Märklin Great Eastern Railway train with Bavarian style tender. *Rear:* Bing Gauge 'O' London and South Western Train. Both *c.* 1902. The coaches have interior fixtures and plaster passengers. Station and lamps by Bing. Figures by William Britain & Sons. Private collection.

Opposite Below
Pre-1900 rowing boat made by Issmayer, a German company better known for small scale-model trains. The boat hull is zinc, the deck tin, the rower brass. The rower's legs are embossed out of the deck. Private collection.

Right
Clockwork car with chauffeur by
Bing. Post-1920. Bethnal Green
Museum, London.

Centre
Two Gauge '1' locomotives by Bing.
The hand-painted Midland Railway
4-4-0, made in 1912, has two speeds.
The 2-4-0 LNWR 'George V' is
lithographed. Private collection.

attachments; and a polished brass boiler with a safety valve, whistle, and water gauge. The attachments for steam engines were even more impressive: a complete smithy with two men at work, and a large stock of toy machinery – circular saws, turning lathes, grindstones, pulleys, and so on. The prices for engines ranged from the Weeden Horizontal Engine at $1.50, and the Weeden Beam Engine at $1.75, to the Large Horizontal No. 10 ('the largest and strongest engine we handle'), which retailed at $8.00. The cheapest of all, the Hero, came down in price over the years until it was selling at a mere twenty cents in the 1900s, evidence that the popularity of steam-driven toys was waning. Even around the turn of the century, steam toys seem to have been doing much less well than solo steam engines. By 1913, Gamages was selling only one steam toy (a motor racing boat), and even such apparently appropriate items as steam rollers and paddle steamers were by then made to be driven by clockwork. One reason for this change is suggested by the number of advertisements published to assure the public that steam-driven toys were 'absolutely safe' with 'not the slightest danger of them bursting'. The very existence of these advertisements hinted that toys of this sort might be hazardous, but this most common explanation for the demise of steam toys is not completely satisfactory. Some boilers were known to overheat, and not every steam toy was as soundly made as it should have been, but these 'unsafe' toys did not disappear after five or ten years when their drawbacks should have been realised, but remained popular for at least another thirty years. Perhaps steam engines no longer seemed worthwhile because steam had ceased to be 'modern' and exciting (although it must be said that real steam trains continued to excite the 'spotter' until they disappeared altogether). Most likely, it was the electric-driven toy, with its improved batteries, and not the clockwork models, that ended the Toy Age of Steam. Still, fashions come and go. 'Hobbies Steam Engines' turned up again at the Army and Navy Stores in 1939, so yet another

Above
Carette Gauge '1' spirit-fired 2-2-0 locomotive, c. 1905-10. Length: 38 cm (15 in). Sotheby's, London.

Below
Bassett-Lowke working model tanker with Stuart electric motor. Length: 74 cm (29 in); and working model tug mounted with binnacle compass, two dinghys, and port and starboard lights. Length: 63.5 cm (25 in). Sotheby's, London.

Right
Carette limousine. 1911. Length:
32 cm (12.8 in). Carette limousines
were made in a variety of sizes and
quality—some with tin tyres, some
with rubber; some hand painted,
some printed. Private collection.

Below
Railway accessories by Bing and
Märklin, 1900-14. Märklin electric
lamp (battery in the base) and train
indicator (for the Dutch market). Bing
station and ticket machine (with real
card tickets). Private collection.

Above
Bing Gauge '1' 0-4-0 hand-painted steam locomotive. *c.* 1902. The train has reciprocating cylinders. Private collection.

resurrection may not be out of the question.

Like other American toymakers, Ives was curiously slow to recognise the appeal of the working scale-model railways. His earliest models (from about the 1880s) were clockwork locomotives that ran without rails, long after Europeans had started to produce complete trains with tracks, sophisticated controls, rolling stock and other accessories. However, once committed to making accurate models, Ives excelled; some features, notably a device to send regular puffs of smoke from the funnels of clockwork locomotives, still arouse the admiration of collectors everywhere.

Ives remained supreme in the United States until the First

World War, and sold toys abroad in some quantity. Still, there was no doubt who the world leader was: American stores – like the French and British – were full of German toys, albeit unlabelled as such, or decked out in other national colours.

The most successful of all the German toymakers was Ernst Paul Lehmann, whose tin can factory began to do better business from 1881 by specialising in tinplate toys. Lehmann's factory was sited in the small town of Brandenburg, on the River Havel, far away from the traditional centres. The only apparent advantage of this location was its proximity to the capital, Berlin, which enabled Lehmann to become even more notable as an exporter than as a

Right
American cold-painted cast-iron clock automaton town crier with a single train movement in his belly. The eyes move with the pendulum. Late 19th cent. Height: 42 cm (16.5 in). Sotheby's, London.

Below
Six cars made between 1900-30: Bing's De Dion (made over a twenty-year period); Hess's Roller; Bing's Tourer; Lehmann's Galop (made over a long period); Gunthermann's Paris-Peking race car; Falk's penny toy racing car. Private collection.

supplier of the home market. This was partly because of all the German makers Lehmann was the most sensitive to foreign tastes, putting out many toys featuring European and American national characteristics, but it was also due to the peculiar qualities of his products which, consistently ingenious in operation, well-finished, and, considering their cheapness, quite remarkably idiosyncratic in design, showed a distinct leaning towards the whimsical and exotic. In particular there were carts of various sorts, driven by clowns or other comic figures, or pulled by zebras, donkeys, ostriches, and other unlikely animals. One long-standing favourite was the Bucking Mule, which almost upset the cart and its clown driver before finally setting off – backwards. Toys of this sort were driven by a clockwork mechanism in the cart, which in fact pushed the animal (or dragged it when it ran backwards). The same principle – reverse engineering – occurs in Lehmann's mysteriously labelled Man Da Rin toy, which has two pigtailed coolies carrying a sedan chair with an imperious mandarin in it: the clockwork is in the chair that drives the coolies. One of the most long-lived Lehmann toys, judging by its inclusion in several decades worth of catalogues, was the Oh-My tap dancer (1903), a rather solemn Negro wearing a battered hat,

Left
Negro clockwork tap dancers. American. 1860. Bethnal Green Museum, London.

Below
Negro Preacher, patented by Excelsior Automatic Toys. American. Height: 25.4 cm (10 in). Connecticut Historical Society.

high collar, checked trousers and spats; he was known for a time (in order to cash in on the craze) as Ragtime Joe, and later still, more brutally, (in the U.S.A.) as the Coon Jigger, or Dancing Nigger.

The Lehmann firm survived two world wars and the death in 1934 of its founder, whose successor, Johann Richter carried on for a time, even after the Second World War. Richter eventually escaped from East Germany to West Germany, and, in 1951, started a new factory at Nuremberg under the Lehmann name and continued a few of the old Lehmann lines. The Lehmann factory still exists in the German Democratic Republic as the VEB Mechanische Spielwaren.

Above
Friction-driven car probably made by Clark. American. *c.* 1900. Bethnal Green Museum, London.

Right
American clockwork figure. *c.* 1890. Probably made by Ives. Christie's, London.

Opposite
Clockwork dancing figures by a member of the Crandall Family. American. 1860–70.

Right
Lehmann's flywheel-driven Duo, mechanical tin rabbit and cart. 1914. Christie's, London.

Above
Althof Bergmann's Jubilee Trotting Course. American. 1876. Blair Whitton collection.

Left
Lehmann's 'Heavy Swell' and Adam the Porter. The lady with the muff is by an unknown German maker. All 1900-14. Private collection.

Right
Box lid from Lehmann's Zikra (or Zebra). Bethnal Green Museum, London.

Below
Right to Left: Kico's Vee Twin; motorcyclist by unknown German maker; Lehmann's clockwork Echo; Lehmann's flywheel-driven Halloh, Gely's single cylinder bike. Private collection.

Left
Toyshop display of Lehmann toys.

Below
Lehmann's Ajax the circus
strongman, patented in 1903. Height:
25.4 cm (10 in). Christie's, London.

Although toymaking was
dominated by the Germans, other
European firms, particularly the
French, proved capable of selling
in quantity at home and abroad,
as is evident from this
advertisement in a January 1877
edition of *New York Fashions*:

> *The mechanical toys imported from*
> *Paris are the finest ever brought to*
> *this country. The figures are*
> *beautiful and correctly costumed,*
> *and the motion is perfect ... The*
> *Saucy Milkmaid is propelled*
> *rapidly around the room, shaking her*
> *head and patting her cow, while the*
> *cow munches oats and lows*
> *contentedly. The Drunken Muleteer*
> *applies the bottle to his mouth with*
> *one hand, and holds on to the mule*
> *with the other. The Murderous*
> *Zouave dashes around the room*
> *furiously snapping a pistol towards*
> *the right, then the left, in a most*
> *reckless manner.*

Not to mention the peasant
pushing his barrow and the New
Gymnast walking on her hands
along a rope. Contemporary
descriptions of Lowther Arcade,
near London's Trafalgar Square,
also make it clear that there were
plenty of French as well as
German mechanical toys in its
shops. Indeed, French
workmanship, especially in ships,
early automobiles and other big
and detailed items, was often
superior to German – but the
prices were more than
proportionately higher. However,
cheap toys *were* made in France as

well, and there was one Parisian
firm, Martin's, producing them
on a large scale.

Fernand Martin, a native of
Amiens, established himself in the
Boulevard de Ménilmontant,
Paris, and for over thirty years
(1878–1912) produced a stream of
new toys, although it must be said
that he was particularly adept at
buying other people's ideas for
next to nothing, or evading patent
regulations by varying the details
of a new invention. In 1909 other
Parisian toymakers were outraged
when Martin presented a
collection of 'his' designs and
inventions to the Conservatoire
des Arts et des Métiers, and a first-
class scandal ensued. Whatever
the rights and wrongs of the case –
most of them impossible to sort
out now – Martin has had the best
of it: the toys are still attributed to
him, and, thanks to his foresight,
the record of his work is more

complete than that of virtually
any other toymaker.

The best-known of all Martin
toys are those nicknamed *les petits
bonshommes Martin* – little
clockwork-driven men and
women dressed in clothes of real
fabric and mostly representing
Parisian types: the messenger-
boy, the concierge, the laundress,
the waiter, the sandwich man, the
gendarme, the advocate. Martin
very cleverly took advantage of
the fact that he could also change
the national character of his toys
by garbing them differently – a
strategically useful ploy for the
export trade. Apart from soldiers,
clowns, acrobats, and various
workers, tradesmen, vehicles, and
animals, Martin made a man
playing bagatelle (a game like
billiards), a bullfighter, a red-
nosed drunkard swigging from a
bottle while swaying dangerously
from side to side, a man catching

Above
Clockwork boat by Ives. American.
1869. Bethnal Green Museum,
London.

Opposite
Cast-iron steam engine with a semi-
circular water chamber mounted on
three legs. Tower holds a walking
beam, one end of which is connected
to a brass piston, the other to a wheel
and pulley. Patented by Russell
Frisbie of Cromwell, Connecticut in
1871 and 1872. Manufactured by J.
& E. Stevens of Cromwell,
Connecticut. Margaret Woodbury
Strong Museum, Rochester.

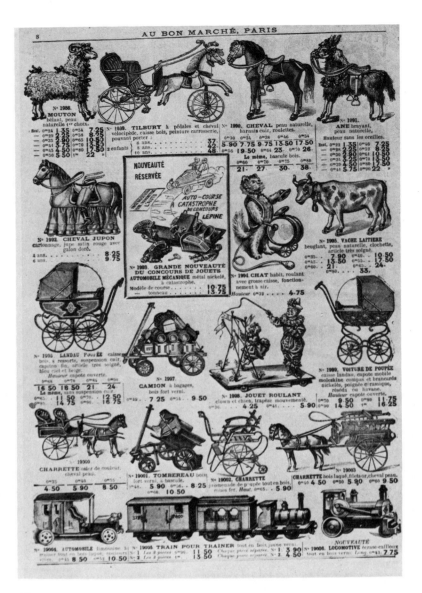

Below
The Log Sawyers (*left*) by Fernand Martin. 1886. Height: 24 cm (9.75 in), and The Mysterious Ball (*right*) by Martin Fernand (invented by M. Gasselin). 1905. Height: 60 cm (24 in). Musée des Arts et Metiers, Paris.

Above
Au Bon Marché 1907 catalogue showing French mechanical toys.

Right
Martin Maréchal Ferrand coloured tin-plate forge. Width: 15.24 cm (6 in). Christie's, London.

a fish and a Dutch girl dropping a
pile of dishes. There were also
various items suggested by current
events or fads such as the Boer
War and the Cake Walk dance,
but the wittiest was a clockwork
horse whose rider, dressed as a
jockey, carried off the *Mona Lisa*,
which in fact was stolen in 1911.
A number of Martin's toys
were friction-driven, and a
surprising number were driven by
the simpler twisted-elastic-band
method. Martin's firm was taken
over by Bonnet et Cie in 1912,
and Martin himself died in 1919,
but some of his models remained
in production until the 1930s.

The leading British firm from
the 1880s was the aptly named
William Britain & Sons. William
Britain himself had been in
business since the 1840s, but the
great years of the firm came much
later – largely, it seems, owing to
the inventive capacities of
William Britain Junior. The
firm's greatest impact on the toy
industry lay in toy-soldier
production. A few years later
they introduced lead soldiers that
were hollow-cast and therefore
lighter and cheaper than any
other kind. This meant a

Above
Billiard player. Clockwork mechanism
in the table. German copy of Martin
toy. 1900. Length: 23.7 cm (9.48 in).
Bethnal Green Museum, London.

Right
Le Gai Violiniste by Fernand Martin.
Late 19th cent. Height: 20 cm (8 in).
Bethnal Green Museum, London.

tremendous expansion in the
market for what British children
used to call 'tin soldiers', but
Britain's also patented and
manufactured their own lines of
mechanical toys until their success
with soldiers and weapons
gradually led them to specialise in
militaria alone. Some of the
earliest examples were quite large
and expensive automata,
probably intended for adult
collectors or shop-window
displays. The Sailor Money Box
was advertised as suitable for
children's savings or as a novelty
item that might attract public
pennies on behalf of some
charitable organisation – which
seems a more likely purpose for a
'toy' costing 27/6 (£1.37½), no

49

mean sum for the pre-First World War period. But then, the sailor (who held out a plate to receive the coin and then tipped it into the money box while raising his hat and bowing) was dressed in satin. Britain's also made other, cheaper toys many of which dealt with currently popular subjects (animals, vehicles, Orientals) and were more solidly made but also more expensive than their German and French counterparts. Britain's, which is still flourishing, seems to have been the first toymaker to apply friction-drive to toys (about 1888). Martin, Lehmann and others quickly followed suit, but the popularity of such toys had largely disappeared in Europe by the beginning of the First World War. They lasted longer in the United States, where the Dayton Friction Toy Works reached the height of its fortunes in 1910 with a friction-powered duck that sold in the tens of thousands. Though less in evidence between the World

Wars, wheel-wind friction toys made something of a come-back in the 1950s.

It is easy to over-sentimentalise the 'Long Edwardian afternoon' before the First World War, though it is perhaps not entirely mistaken to regret the passing of what seems to have been a more stable and secure order. The impression of ease and prosperity is, of course, a partial one since these benefits were not widely distributed, but for those who were able to partake, there was an unprecedented abundance and variety of good things to be had.

Gamage's 1913 *Christmas Bazaar* catalogue gives a significant indication of this abundance before the fall, with over a hundred pages of toys, dolls, games, novelties and jokes, both British and foreign made. Although makers and places of origin are not mentioned, it is not difficult to pick out Lehmann's Oh My or Ragtime Joe; Britain's Equestrienne (a horse running in

Above

Right: Lehmann's tin Oh-My tapdancer, known in the United States as the Alabama Coon Jigger. Made from before 1914 up until the 1930s. *Left:* Lehmann's Li-La, otherwise known as The Autosisters. The women beat the dog and the dog tries to get away. 1900-04. Private collection.

Far Right

William Britain & Sons' The Walking Elephant. The flywheel-drive mechanism is worked by turning the parasol. William Britain & Sons collection.

Right

William Britain & Sons' The General. *c.* 1880. The friction-drive mechanism is operated by spinning the umbrella. The right hand originally wielded a sword which was thrust forward when the toy was set in motion. Museum of London.

a circle, carousel fashion, while its lady rider leaps over a bar); and a version of Martin's bagatelle game, here wrongly renamed the Mechanical Billiard Table. There are clockwork or friction-driven clowns, cyclists, acrobats, mice (seven times cheaper than the mice of the 1850s), rats, railway porters, lobsters, geese, ducks, horses, donkeys, tigers, beetles, spring-heeled jacks, skittle alleys, loop-the-loop courses and mountain railways; there is even a clockwork 'varsity rowing eight in a boat, available in the Oxford or Cambridge colours'. The range of

trains is enormous, as is that of ships, which included clockwork torpedo boats, gun boats, dreadnoughts, destroyers, submarines (alternately diving and rising to the surface as the clockwork changed the angle of the fins on the sub's body), fire boats, ocean liners, paddle steamers, tug-boats, yachts – and seaplanes, at this date evidently regarded as more nautical than aeronautical. The accuracy of the aeroplane and automobile sections is striking in view of the fact that both forms of transport were less than twenty years old,

Opposite
Page from Gamage's 1913 Christmas Bazaar catalogue.

Below Left
William Britain & Sons' clockwork cyclist thought to represent the French tightrope walker, Charles Blondin. 1888. William Britain & Sons collection.

Below Right
William Britain & Sons' Equestrienne. Christie's, London.

Bottom
Clockwork tin fire engine. English. Bethnal Green Museum, London.

53

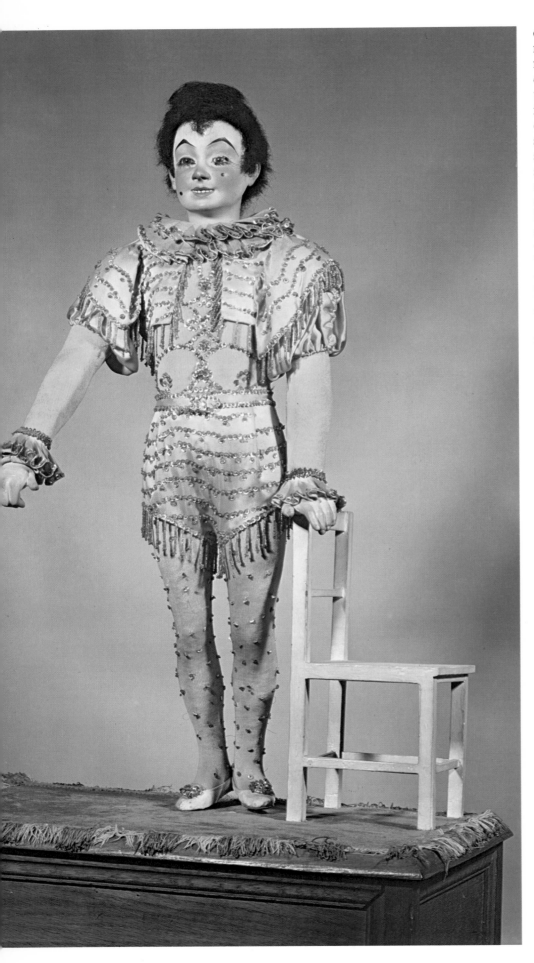

even in the adult world. Flying model aircraft was evidently a rich boy's hobby: some examples cost as much as ten pounds, and the number of accessories on sale is quite remarkable by 1913 and even modern standards. The car section is informative even from a social history point of view, showing the extent to which the automobile had become part of ordinary daily life. As well as limousines, tourers and racing cars, there are workaday delivery vans, lorries, tip-trucks, motor buses and taxi cabs. The star item was the 'Double Torpedo Phaeton Motor Car with powerful clockwork spring, and fitted brake . . . made to run backwards and forwards, also straight or circular by means of lever in car. Finely enamelled.' It is listed at a price of 22/6 or 32/6 (£1.62$\frac{1}{2}$). By contrast, the poor child could hope for a garage with opening doors and two clockwork cars, sold by the same store for 1/32 of the Phaeton's price – that is, one shilling. Relative values were so different in those days that almost any statement about prices can be misleading, but it seems relevant to note that at least a third of all male workers earned less than the price of a Phaeton every week, and that for female labourers the shilling clockwork cars and garage with opening doors represented the price of a day-and-a-half's work. The same shilling, incidentally, bought two glasses of draught champagne in one of London's West End saloons.

That, too, was part of the stable, ordered world before the War.

Left
Cha-U-Kao. Life-sized performing acrobat by Vichy. *c.* 1876. Private collection.

Opposite
Pierrot with musical movement serenading the moon. By Vichy. 19th cent. Sotheby's, London.

Sand, Air, Balance, Torsion, and Tension Toys

Although most of the objects discussed so far, those worked by clockwork, friction-drive, levers, or, especially, steam, were certainly the most intriguing novelty toys to have been produced in the eighteenth and nineteenth centuries, other methods, which had been developed centuries before, were also used.

One of the simplest forces employed to produce movement was the sand motor, based solely on the properties of fine sand and the law of gravity. With its flow controlled on the hour-glass principle, the sand trickles steadily from its container onto a miniature paddle-wheel, driving it round and providing the impulse to turn the sails of a toy windmill or to power some similar object. The principle, which has been known since ancient times, was used in the seventeenth century to power the movements of an elaborate peepshow given to seven-year-old Louis XIII. For all we know, Egyptian children may have had some sort of sand-and-gravity-driven toys since the Egyptians had sand clocks and hour glasses, but the first natural force on record as having been harnessed for the amusement of the young is air. Several medieval pictures show children carrying little toys with whirling arms that worked on the 'windmill' principle, and children

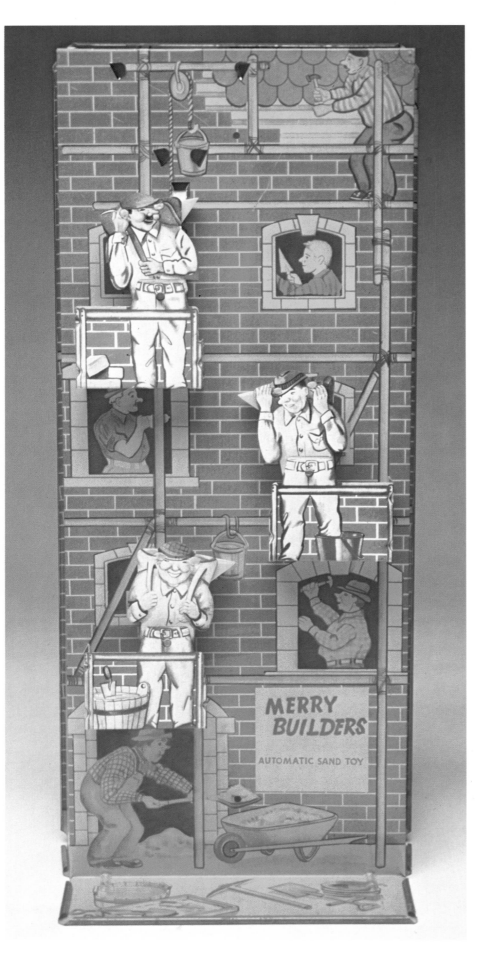

have played with miniature versions of the windmill itself for about two centuries, these toys reaching the height of their popularity during the Victorian era. Surviving sand toys date from the nineteenth century, when their attraction was the relative cheapness of the mechanism.

Around 1800, sets of paper cut-outs, sold in France, could be made up into sand toys with paddle wheels, but the most popular type of sand toys consisted of picture backgrounds with little sand-driven figures attached, their jointed limbs performing more or less complex set pieces. When the action ended, the box or toy had to be turned upside down (and/or round and round) so that the sand trickled back into its container. The majority of sand pictures were of whimsical or sentimental subjects – kittens, monkeys, organ grinders. Most were German-made, but there were French sand pictures (one commemorating the 1851 Exhibition) as well as British and American examples. In the hands of children, sand pictures were even more accident-prone than clockwork toys, and by the 1880s they were no longer made. Easily the most successful sand toy of the twentieth century, patented in the United States in 1909 and manufactured at first by the Sand Toy Company of Pittsburg, was Sandy Andy, a wheeled tip-car that received sand from a hopper at the top of a chute and then rolled down the chute to dump the load into a box or lorry. This simple toy survived two world wars and is still being made and sold somewhere in one form or another, one example of which is the modern 'Merry Builders' sand toy.

Other, more ingenious toys have been made to utilise the fact that air rises when it is heated, one example of which was a replica of the hot-air balloon that was operated by placing a fire beneath the open bottom so that the rising heat lifted it into the sky. The very first real ascent,

masterminded by the Montgolfier brothers in 1783, touched off the ensuing balloon mania. Toy versions, sold or made at home, must have been powered by spirit-soaked wads of rag, but the subsequent hydrogen balloons, which proved safer for aviators, were more dangerous for child-experimenters. Nevertheless, in the early years of the twentieth century, when the achievements of Count Zeppelin and Santos-Dumont made airships as exciting as planes, Märklin sold accurate lighter-than-air models that flew when filled with hydrogen – presumably made with the help of a chemistry kit.

More homely applications of the same principle were the figures, manufactured of sheet tin, that were wired to stoves and driven by the rising heat. Most of the figures went through the motions of working at home or in the workshop, but there were a smaller number of fiddlers and acrobats. These toys, popular in nineteenth-century America, seem imbued with the spirit of that time and place, and it is likely that the hot air toy was regarded as an attractive decoration in many a remote rural farmhouse. (Riley Ives, father of the more famous Edward, made hot air toys of this type in the 1860s.) Whether moved by air currents or rising heat, the modern 'mobile' that hangs from the ceiling is in the

Above
Right: Lehmann's Luna. The balloon rises when the string is pulled. Issued 1900-14. *Left:* The Santos balloon marketed by Moko celebrated the Brazilian Santos Dumont's circling of the Eiffel Tower by balloon. Private collection.

Left
The tightrope walker is a balance toy and has an elegantly decorated counter-weight. The clockwork clown on the pig rocks backwards and forwards as he holds the pig's ears. German. *c.* 1900. Private collection.

Above
American hot-air toy. Museum of London.

Opposite Top
Page from Gamage's 1913 Christmas Bazaar catalogue showing a variety of spinning tops and gyroscopic toys.

Opposite Bottom
An elastic-band powered penny farthing that circles its central pivot. The boy with the hoop, made c. 1875, originally had a clockwork mechanism. Probably French. Private collection.

same tradition. Appropriately enough, the American artist Alexander Calder, who fathered the concept of mobiles, was also a toymaker.

Air pressure is another motive force. In its most basic form, it is used to work the pop-gun, but the most direct of all air-powered toys are the ones moved by blowing down a tube: the air flows round a horizontal wheel making the little figures perched on it dance. In a more imposing Japanese version, whirling wooden 'fists' on the end of strings were made to strike a drum.

Weights, gravity and balance have also been used in toys in various permutations, for example, the shifting weights that pull acrobatic figures down one step after another, head over heels and heels over head. One of the most entertaining versions was 'Slinky', essentially a large spring, which slithered from step to step like a rather bouncy eel. Conversely, toys like the Tilting Doll, Fanny Royd, Tombola or Roly-Poly can be knocked right over, but always swing straight back on to their loaded bases; and in toys with swinging weights under them, movement is transferred from one part to another – pecking chickens seem to be a children's favourite. In other balance toys, figures fixed by pivots on to a stable background are counter weighted so that they swing forward and backwards, such as the 'galloping horses' toy, the most basic example, and such as the German-made 'Das Komische Pärchen' ('The Comic Couple') an elaborate kit with interchangeable parts. The latter example, made in 1860, consists of the figures of a man and a woman who can appear in a variety of grotesque ways by permutating a stock of heads and hats that is part of the kit. The manufacturer of this toy clearly believed in its export potential labelling it in German, English, French and Italian as Common Market Style.

Movement can also be obtained by creating and then releasing tension. The Jack-in-the-Box and similar toys, which have been popular for centuries, delighting children and shortening the lives of elderly ladies and gentlemen, are operated by a simple device: a figure attached to a compressed spring leaps out when the spring is released by opening the box. In characteristic style, Charles Dickens took hold of the malevolent aspect of such 'surprise' toys in *The Cricket on the Hearth*, making it manifest in an evil toymaker:

whose soul perfectly revelled [in] appalling masks; hideous, hairy, red-eyed Jacks in Boxes; Vampire Kites; demoniacal Tumblers who wouldn't lie down, and were perpetually flying forward, to stare infants out of countenance [and similar grotesqueries].

Torsion accumulates force in a similar way – most effectively in toys using an elastic band that is twisted round and round without allowing a release of tension at either end; when finally released, the band's unwinding provides a strong, if relatively brief, impulse. This can carry a toy through the air, and must have been the principle behind a good many flying toys like Bob the Bat, with which Lewis Carroll used to entertain some of the children who visited him in his rooms at Christ Church. According to Isa Bowman's *The Story of Lewis Carroll* (1899):

[Bob] had many adventures. There was no way of controlling the direction of its flight, and one morning, a hot summer's morning, when the window was wide open, Bob flew out into the garden and alighted in a bowl of salad which a scout [Oxford college servant] was taking to someone's rooms. The poor fellow was so startled by the sudden flapping apparition that he dropped the bowl, and it was broken into a thousand pieces.

Although some late eighteenth-century toys were based on torsion, its most interesting

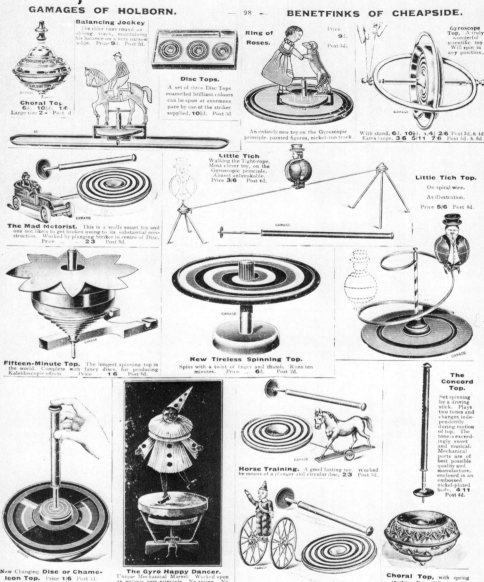

(Catalogue illustrations with labels: Balancing Jockey; Choral Top; Disc Tops; Ring of Roses; Gyroscope Top; The Mad Motorist; Little Tich Walking the Tight-rope; Little Tich Top; Fifteen-Minute Top; New Tireless Spinning Top; The Concord Top; New Changing Disc or Chameleon Top; The Gyro Happy Dancer; Horse Training; Balancing Clown. Disc Top; Choral Top with spring starter.)

position: depending on the area of the disc pushed, the cat bent its head, leant to one side, made its tail go rigid, or fell into a state of utter collapse.

The skipjack was another simple torsion-propelled toy that was usually made at home. It consisted of a wishbone, the 'prong' ends of which were linked by a piece of string or elastic. A wooden pin was then attached across the string and turned over and over, 'winding up' the line. One end of the pin could be stuck to the joint of the wishbone with a substance, such as wax, that would hold it in place, but only for a limited time. Meanwhile, the owner of the skipjack could leave it in the way of some unsuspecting relative, who would be startled when, the pin having forced its way through the wax, the toy started to skip about the room.

Tops and other gyroscopic toys exploit the principle of inertia, which would keep them moving for ever at a constant speed if they spun on a perfectly level surface and in a vacuum instead of our impeding atmosphere. Since the late nineteenth century, gyroscopic toys have from time to time been made on the carousel principle – a plunger spinning a flat wheel which carries round with it (for example) a horse on a wheel, or a wobbly 'Mad Motorist'.

application was to toy aeroplanes and gliders in the age of the Wright Brothers and Louis Bleriot, when the only convincing way of making a toy or model aircraft fly (unless one spent a small fortune on models driven by compressed air) was with twisted elastic bands.

Another amusing item that exploited the qualities of elastic was a small figure, such as a cat, made up of a dozen or so separate parts threaded through with an elastic and standing on a small pedestal. When the disc at the base of the pedestal was pushed, relaxing the elastic, various parts of the cat's body changed

Left
A variety of spinning tops. Märklin's butterflies and dragonflies spin when the plunger is attached and then pushed down. German. 1920-30; the Dessy top revolves around a variety of shapes; Lehmann's Gnom and Hop-Hop, mechanically operated, bounce and spin. German. 1900-14; German mechanical humming tops. 1900-14; American mechanical spinning tops; Fountain top and other with unknown action by William Britain & Sons. c. 1900; French optical spinning tops. 1890-1900; English Melton top. 1950s; Ballerina top with rack-operated gyroscope in her skirt. German. 1930s. Private collection.

Below
Tumbling clowns with mercury mechanisms. The Chinamen are German. c. 1850. The other clown is English. c. 1900. Bethnal Green Museum, London.

P. 62

Mechanical Banks and Bell Toys

Left to Right
Group of mechanical cast-iron moneybanks: Punch and Judy bank, patented in 1884 in Buffalo, New York, height: 17.78 cm (7 in); the Lilliput bank, patented in 1875; the Magic bank, patented in 1873 and in 1876. Private collection.

In the nineteenth century, when Europe was famous for tinplate, American firms became the outstanding manufacturers of iron toys. Two factors which probably contributed to this development were the decreased demand for iron after the Civil War: with the armaments boom over, some foundries turned to toy production to keep their machines working; and, at the same time, the fact that home production was favoured by protective tariffs making foreign iron and steel more expensive.

The most well-known of all cast iron toys are the brightly painted mechanical banks that perform some amusing action when a coin is deposited. They are essentially American toys, displaying the nineteenth-century American fondness for humorous caricatures of contemporary figures and references to current events; and only in the United States were they produced in such quantity and variety. They were tremendously popular from the 1870s to the turn of the century, and only ceased being made around 1920.

The leading manufacturer of mechanical banks was the J. & E. Stevens Company of Cromwell, Connecticut, which had been turning out quantities of toy wheels, irons, garden tools and pistols even before the Civil War. The Stevens Company, like the Ives firm, was particularly successful at hiring talented inventors who came up with one new model after another.

The early Stevens mechanical banks developed from static money boxes made to look more or less like actual bank buildings, a type which was popular in the 1880s. The production processes included all the steps appropriate to making a bronze statuette – wax model, plaster of paris casts, filing and chasing – at the end of which the bronze served as a model for the eventual cast-iron product. The mechanical principle was introduced by J. Hall of Watertown, Massachusetts, an inventor who patented the bank in 1869. Early examples of this type include the Cashier Bank, with a cashier who jumped through the roof to take the coin; and the Magic Bank, with a cashier in a doorway fronted by a shelf on which the coin was laid: when a knob at the side was pressed, the cashier and shelf swung round, disappearing with the coin. The Lilliput Bank, which was smaller and more ornate, operated similarly. Almost all the mechanical banks were operated by one, or at most two, levers that moved ingenious combinations of push or release mechanisms, but a very few banks incorporated spring-driven elements. Among these were an

Right
The Tammany cast-iron bank. Patented in 1873 and 1875. The figure is supposed to represent Boss Tweed. Sometimes called the Little Fat Man bank. Bethnal Green Museum, London.

Below
The Indian Shooting Bear bank. Patented by J. & E. Stevens of Cromwell, Connecticut in 1888. A paper cap can be inserted in the gun so that when the hammer hits the end of the gun, a realistic gunshot is heard as the coin is flung into the bear's stomach. Bethnal Green Museum, London.

amazingly ornate 'Jumping Rope Bank', with a little girl skipping, quite worthy of the 1851 Great Exhibition in London, and a Race-Course Bank with a horse-and-buggy race round a circuit. The Novelty Bank was more notable for its catalogue description than for its mechanism: the bank facade swung away to reveal:

a gentlemanly cashier [who has] an iron constitution, [has] never known fatigue or impatience, and [who] deposits the money where even he himself cannot again meddle with it, and hence will never be a defaulting cashier.

Stevens started manufacturing the banks at the height of the New York City Tammany Hall scandals, when 'Boss Tweed' and his ring were exposed for grand larceny. Stevens's Tammany Bank, 'Tweed', which became immensely popular, consisted of a suave-looking man with a mustache, who sat with his hand out; when given a coin, he rapidly transferred it to his breast pocket, nodding urbanely as he did so. Long after Tweed had been forgotten by most people, Stevens continued to sell the bank, re-named the Fat Man Bank, which remained in demand until mechanical banks in general began to lose their appeal.

The slogans covering the Breadwinner's Bank attach it more specifically to its 1880s and '90s origins, a time of intense labour unrest. A worker, equipped with a hammer and standing over a large and rather uninviting mound of 'Honest Labour Bread', confronts the villainous monopolist, with his swag bag labelled 'Boodle Steal Bribery'; underneath is the legend 'Send the Rascals Up' – that is, send the monopolists to prison. A long anvil-like object which the monopolist grasps with both hands is labelled 'Monpoly' (a mis-spelling for which there seems to be no plausible explanation); the coin is placed on it, the activating lever is pressed, the hammer falls, the coin is flung

Above
The William Tell bank. Patented by J. & E. Stevens in 1896. A paper cap can be inserted so that a gunshot is heard as the coin is shot into the castle and knocks the apple off the boy's head. Private collection.

Below
The Trick Dog cast-iron bank. Patented in 1888. When a coin is placed in the dog's mouth, the dog jumps through the hoop and drops the coin in the barrel. Length: 21 cm (8.4 in). Private collection.

into the Breadwinner's Bank, and the see-sawing 'anvil' shoots the monopolist into the air – literally 'sending the rascal up'.

The Chinaman was another current affairs bank that was entertaining despite the puzzling significance of its performance. The pigtailed, smiling Chinaman lay on a log until the coin was deposited; then he showed a handful of playing cards (all aces) and saluted, while a rat ran out of the log. It is generally supposed that this refers in some way to the question of Chinese immigration in the late 1800s.

A later mechanical bank with a nice extra feature was the Artillery Bank:

made wholly of iron, highly finished and bronzed throughout. Cannon (or mortar) is brass plated; tower and artillerymen, Japanese bronze. Place the coin in the mortar, push back the hammer and press the thumbpiece and the coin is fired into the fort or tower. Paper caps can be used if desired.

Which they no doubt were. The Artillery Bank, like the less exciting U.S. Navy Bank with

swivelling guns, was produced by Stevens in response to the Spanish-American War of 1898.

One of the Spanish-American war slogans, 'Remember the *Maine*!' (the *U.S.S. Maine* was a battleship that blew up in Havana harbour on 15 February 1898) was used – even a few years later – to advertise an iron *Battleship Bank*. The Sinking Battleship, made by the Walbert Manufacturing Company of Chicago, actually broke in two and sank when struck by a rubber torpedo.

The war also made a national hero of future U.S. president Theodore ('Teddy') Roosevelt, whose burly, bespectacled appearance and passion for outdoor sports was taken up by caricaturists and toymakers alike. One of the Stevens banks is Teddy and the Bear, in which Roosevelt is about to shoot a bear whose head is poking out of a hollow tree trunk. It was probably inspired by the famous incident that led to the invention of the Teddy Bear,

but Teddy and the Bear was only a topical variation on a basic situation – man shoots at target – that was exploited again and again. The original and probably the best of these was the Creedmore Bank of 1877, devised for Stevens by the inventive Mr. Bowen. This showed a soldier about to fire his rifle at a target tacked onto a tree trunk. The coin was placed on the rifle barrel; then a touch on the soldier's foot flung it into the slot in the centre of the target. In this model, too, a paper cap could be fixed on to the rifle so that there was a bang when the soldier 'fired'.

One of the most ornate banks was put out by Stevens to celebrate the four-hundredth anniversary of Christopher Columbus's voyage across the Atlantic. The Columbus Bank came in a variety of colours and was embellished with relief scenes as well as moving figures. It was activated by placing a coin at Columbus's feet and pressing a lever: the coin disappeared, and,

when an Indian popped out from
a log and proffered a pipe of
peace, Columbus saluted him.

Many of the banks were
humorous in appeal, exploiting
animal characteristics, sports and
outdoor hobbies, or other
activities that interested children:
a baby frog that kicks a coin into
his mother's mouth; a bad-
tempered mule that kicks up his
hind legs, flinging his rider
forwards and dislodging and
depositing the coin (caption: 'I
always did 'spise a mule'); baby
eagles that rise from their nests in
hope of being fed, the mother
eagle, with the coin in her beak,
bending forward to drop it into
the nest; a guide-dog that takes
his blind master's coin and
deposits it; a boat that slides down
a chute and knocks the coin into
the bank; football players who
collide; a baseball pitcher who
hurls the coin, the batter striking
and missing, the catcher catching
and depositing the coin; an
acrobat who swings on a
horizontal bar, kicking a clown so
that he stands on his head and in
doing so, knocks the coin into the
bank; and so on. Some were very
simple, like the the Owl and Frog
banks: one gulp and the coin is
gone, others quite impressively
complicated: the Bad Accident
Bank, for example, involving a
boy running in front of a cart
pulled by a donkey: the donkey
rears up, almost upsetting the
rider and cart.

Outside the United States,
interest was very limited,
although a few American models
were adapted to British
idiosyncrasies, such as the
Association Football bank, dating
from the 1880s, which consisted of
a shorts-clad player kicking the
coin into a latticed box. However,
by 1913, any British vogue that
mechanical banks had ever
enjoyed was over: in the 100-odd
pages of Gamage's *Christmas
Bazaar* catalogue there is not a
single example; the closest
approximation is the Taxi Bank,
which merely registered the
amount saved on the taxi's meter.

The impression given by the catalogues is that, from about 1900, register banks were steadily gaining in popularity at the expense of the older types of mechanical bank.

About the ugliest of all the banks is one that celebrates Peary's conquest of the North Pole in 1909: the bank itself is a shapeless lump, and the crude little figures on it would do no credit to child, lunatic or primitive art. Its sole virtue is the simple mechanism by which a coin placed in the slot raises the United States flag above the bank. Nevertheless, the sheer rarity of this piece has made it quite valuable.

Revived interest in mechanical banks has led to revived production, though in lighter, cheaper materials than cast iron. In particular, real – or perhaps one should say adult – banks have grasped that the miniature form is a good advertisement. Hence, for example, the gleaming gilded space rocket, resting on its fins and pointing at the stars, that exhorts its owner to 'Aim to save at Newton Savings Bank.'

A cast iron toy that outlasted even the mechanical bank in popularity was the bell toy, which chimed as it – and often also the figures on it – moved about. The

catalogue description of one which was both bank and bell toy read:

Iron organ bank . . . , elegantly finished, large chimes of bells, dancing figures revolve when the handle is turned, the monkey deposits the coin in the vault and politely raises his hat . . . This bank is too heavy to go by mail.

The bell toy was another essentially American novelty, closely associated with the area around the town of New Hampton, Connecticut. By the middle of the nineteenth century, firms in the area were producing a great range of bells, gongs and rattles. One such firm, the Gong Bell Manufacturing Company, began to specialise in rattles and bells for children; the early toys being only simple bells, mounted on the axle between a pair of wheels, that rang when the toy was rolled along the floor. Then, in the mid 1880s, the Gong Bell Company began to produce animated bell toys, as did the N. N. Hill Brass Company which set up in East Hampton, New York, in 1889.

Animated bell toys worked on the same principle as the earliest bell toys; that is, bell and movements were activated by the turning of the wheels. In most cases each revolution rings the

bell and simultaneously causes some simple action to occur, for example Jonah popping in and out of the Whale's mouth at each chime. J. & E. Stevens made a Columbus Bell Toy that relied solely on the appeal of its ringing bell and unusually profuse ornament, 'handsomely painted in bronze and fancy colours'. The design represents an ancient state barge manned by oarsmen, with Columbus in the bow – for reasons obscure, since Columbus would never have made it across the Atlantic in a state barge, however handsomely painted.

The most impressive of the wheel-driven toys were those with performing animals, like the lion jumping through a hoop held by a clown, and the elephant swaying from side to side with the bell rope held in his trunk, so that the strikers on each end of the rope hit the bell in front of him. There were plenty of other circus and animal characters, and versions with popular comic characters such as the Captain and the (Katzenjammer) kids; or the fire engine with galloping wheel-bellied horses and alarm gong, which was a much more elaborate and expensive item. Other more typical bell toys had animals or

WANTED — TOYS

Above Right
Variety of American bell toys. 19th cent.

Above Left
The Monkey and The Cocoanut bank. American. Patented by Bowen in 1886. When a coin is placed on the monkey's head, he drops it into the opening cocoanut and his eyes roll. Private collection.

Left
The bulldog bank. American. Patented by James H. Bowen in 1880. When a coin is placed on the dog's nose and his tail is then pulled, the dog's jaw shoots forward to catch the coin and drop it into the bank in his stomach. Private collection.

Opposite
The English Footballer bank. Patented 1900. Museum of Childhood, Edinburgh.

Right
The Jonah and the Whale mechanical cast-iron bank. Patented in 1890. Jonah tosses the coin from his tray towards the whale, and the whale opens its mouth to gulp down the coin. Private collection.

Below
Cast-iron bell toy consisting of a grey horse pulling a chariot of green leaves with a seat in the form of an open lavender rose. A parasol-shaped bell is above the rose. A boy with a red shirt and blue trousers sits on the horse's back. Manufactured by the Gong Bell Manufacturing Co., of East Hampton, Connecticut. *c.* 1890. Margaret Woodbury Strong Museum, Rochester.

Bottom
A bell toy with Punch sitting at one end and a boy holding a cat at the other end. The sides of the well in the centre are marked 'Ding Dong Bell, Pussy's not in the Well'. The bell is under the roof of the well. Made by the Gong Bell Manufacturing Co., of East Hampton, Connecticut. *c.* 1900. Margaret Woodbury Strong Museum, Rochester.

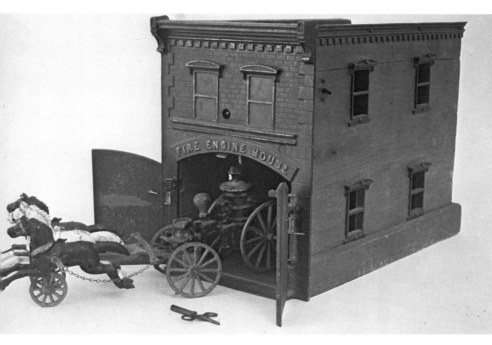

fish lunging for bait they never quite succeeded in reaching; and, to maintain a balance of human-animal advantage, a hunter who never quite succeeded in shooting the rabbit before it disappeared into a hole.

Fewer bell toys than mechanical banks reflected contemporary events. The Spanish-American War raised the fiercest passions, with Teddy Roosevelt and the Rough Riders charging up the San Juan Hill to chimes, and Uncle Sam beating up the Don on a platform 'ornamented with the American flag, head of an eagle, stars, and painted in patriotic colours'. Apparently the Gong Bell Company later used virtually the same pair as the Cossack and the Jap when the Russo-Japanese war broke out in 1905.

It is difficult to enthuse about some of these toys, despite the verve and intelligence that went into making them: Jolly Niggers and Coons, and Uncle Sams beating up Dons, represent a world that should have been left behind long ago. Better to remember these toys by the quaint folk humour we should prefer to have survived: for example, the Baby Quieter Wheel Toy, in which a gentleman sits flourishing his *Evening News* and holding one leg up in the air, with a baby perched on it: 'as it is drawn, each revolution of the wheel rings the bell and jumps the baby'.

Mechanical and Musical Dolls

Mechanical dolls play only a small and recent part in the long history of dolls. Doll-like objects are among the earliest known representational artifacts, although the voluptuous 'Venus' statuettes of 25,000 B.C. are more likely to have been fertility symbols than toys. Whether as toys or funerary objects, hand-made dolls accompanied Egyptian children and adults into the afterlife; without any doubt they served girls in ancient Greece as playthings; and they appear in dozens of other cultures as fetishes, ceremonial offerings, souvenirs, and toys, but it wasn't until the nineteenth century that dolls, like other toys, mechanical or not, were made in large quantities and for an intended juvenile market.

As for other toys, doll fashions changed over the years. The earliest record of a North American doll, depicted in one of the coloured drawings done by John White in the years after 1585 on Roanoake Island, is of an Indian chief's wife, daughter, and

Wax composition doll with sleeping eyes which are operated by wires that protrude from the body. The same mechanism operates the tongue movement. English. 1860s. Height: 60.96 cm (24 in). Bethnal Green Museum, London.

the daughter's unmistakably European doll, dressed in the plumed hat, high shoulders and flaring coat of the soberly respectable Englishman.

In the 1840s there was a fashion for china dolls with heads of glazed porcelain which could be very pretty but rarely avoided a certain gleaming, cherubic unreality. Only a few years later, a new kind of wax doll, one that was relatively cheap, became popular in Britain and was taken up on the Continent. The head of this doll was actually made of painted papier mâché with a wax coating, giving the doll a smooth, transparent complexion. The rage for each of these two types of doll was brief, but they remained standard items of production, selling steadily for several generations.

As in so many branches of toymaking, German doll makers led the world in the nineteenth century, the most important centre being Sonneberg in Thuringia (now part of the G.D.R.) which had by then been linked with doll making for well over five hundred years. Other doll-making centres included Neustadt, Coburg and Gotha, all of them also in Thuringia, but there was a break in German supremacy between the 1860s and 1880s, when Parisian firms marketed superbly made, beautifully dressed, and extremely expensive luxury dolls which the Germans themselves could not rival except by direct imitation.

Above
Sleeping Twins. The eyes are connected to wires that protrude at the sides of the hips. German. Mid-19th cent. Bethnal Green Museum, London.

Right
Autoperipatetikos doll and box. American. 1862. German parian bust with black moulded hair and kid arms. Mauve silk dress covers a cardboard bell inside which is the mechanism. When wound, a bar is lowered down each brass foot in turn and causes the doll to be propelled forward. Worthing Museum and Art Gallery.

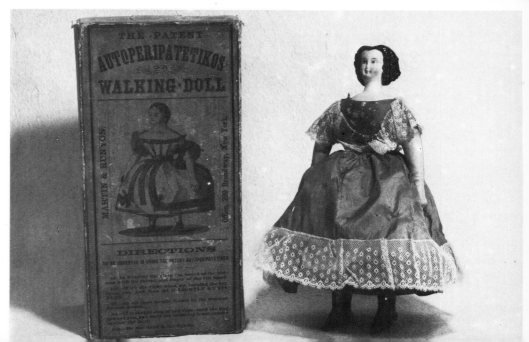

At first these were made of glazed porcelain, but it was found that better results were obtained with *bisque* – biscuit, or unglazed porcelain. (It is often wrongly called parian, which was a kind of biscuit developed in the nineteenth century to resemble marble.) The Parisian firms exploited detailed modelling of *bisque*, but although their taste ran to idealised prettiness rather than realistic accuracy, the achieved matt 'skin' gave the face a naturalness and warmth lacking in the glazed-type heads.

The most famous of the French doll makers was Jumeau, whose factory was on the outskirts of Paris, at Montreuil. Jumeau has often been credited with inventing the luxury doll, or *poupée de luxe*, but there is no real evidence for this attribution except for Jumeau's indisputable eminence. Similarly, he has been credited with devising the new doll's body of the 1880s, which was the first to have the now familiar ball-and-socket joints held together by strong elastic; it soon became apparent that this was both the simplest and most efficient method of giving dolls movable, properly articulated members.

The new body was used for a new type of doll. This was the *bébé* – who was, however, not a baby at all, but a little girl. The change was a slight but definite one which can be summed up as the little-girlish lady (*poupée*) losing much of her popularity to the little-lady-like girl (*bébé*). The *bébé* had a chubbier, more toddler-like face, but she too was dressed in the height of Second Empire and

Opposite
Wax composition sleeping doll with eyes which open and close. German. *c.* 1850. Bethnal Green Museum, London.

Right
The American Girl musical doll. Head by Jumeau. Body by Leopold Lambert. English. Height: 60 cm (24 in). Private collection.

Belle Epoque adult fashion – with hat, parasol, fur wrap, jewellery and modish coats and dresses.

Supplying clothes and equipment for Parisian dolls was a small industry on its own. Miniature high-fashion clothing was made with the same kind of skill and care associated with its life-sized equivalents; in addition, there were scale versions of personal goods from soap to stationery, furniture, houses, vehicles, and so on. Mechanical items included some we have already come across in other contexts, but there were also some incredible luxury pieces, the *chef d'oeuvre* being a lavatory that actually flushed.

Apart from Jumeau, there were also many other doll makers, including some whose existence is known through their anonymous products alone, but one other well known one, Jumeau's great rival (a posthumous rival at least, since it is difficult to verify the contemporary standing vis-a-vis the famous Jumeau), was the firm founded by Leon Casimir Bru.

Modern connoisseurs are divided between the two in their allegiances, with a majority probably now inclined to place Bru above Jumeau, but in terms of their dolls' facial appearance, preference is largely a matter of taste. The Jumeau *bébés* had a slightly more intelligent appearance than the Bru dolls which, with their wide-eyed and open-mouthed look, were more old-fashioned although perhaps also more craftsmanlike in their construction methods.

In general improvements were rarely the work of a single man or country. As has been seen with the history of other toys, a particular firm might patent an idea, or a particular nation come to dominate the market, but often enough these were the result of researches carried out by several generations of craftsmen working in different countries. This is no less applicable to the development of walking and/or talking dolls. As was true for craftsmen like de Vaucanson and Jaquet-Droz, whose creations can legitimately

Above Left
Autoperipatetikos dolls and boxes. *Left and right:* made by Martin & Runyon of New York. Height: 25.2 cm (10 in). *Centre:* Porcelain-headed doll with mechanism. Bethnal Green Museum, London.

Above Right
Autoperipatetikos doll, the Walking Zouave, invented by Enoch Rich Morrison. 1862. Height: 25 cm (10 in). Estelle A. Winthrop collection.

Right

Two walking dolls by Steiner of Paris. Both *c.* 1880. French. Both dolls have a *'Maman'/'Papa'* talking mechanism. The doll on the left has a single action drive-wheel and variable front steering wheel which determines the direction the doll walks in. Height: 38.1 cm (15 in). The doll on the right has a clockwork mechanism that causes it to move its head from side to side, to swing its arms, and walk. Height: 46.99 cm (18.5 in). Bethnal Green Museum, London.

Below

Walking Doll. French. *c.* 1880. Head turns to one side, arms move up and down, legs move backwards and forwards and the doll utters a cry. Steiner mechanism. Height: 45.72 cm (18 in). Worthing Museum and Art Gallery.

be described as the precursors of mechanical dolls, here too the problem was to make the clockwork mechanism smaller, simpler and cheaper. The earlier examples were fairly bulky, and the doll had to wear a long dress to cover the mechanism and the wheels on which it ran. One example of this type is the 'Autoperipatetikos' doll that was marketed in 1863 by the American firm of Martin and Bunyan. She could step out on her own two feet, but needed a full crinoline to cover her substantial clockwork mechanism, which was advanced enough to make her an American export to the toymaking nations of Europe. She even appeared in a number of different guises, and on occasion changed sex, for example to become a dashing Zouave – a type of French infantryman with conveniently baggy trousers. In dolls with more complicated and efficient works, levers pushed one leg in front of the other, the doll's balance ensured by her being shod in heavy metal or, like other

toys, placed behind a cart which she pushed forward.

Like the life-sized automata of the eighteenth century, most of the nineteenth-century talking dolls were operated by the manipulation of some outside attachment, the most common being a tube attached to a hollow rubber ball that, when squeezed, activated the mechanism. There is some evidence that a bellows mechanism was used at about 1760 in England to make a crying doll, but if so, this was a false start. Speaking dolls were developed slowly, presumably because the combination of a miniature mechanism and consonantal sounds was difficult to achieve – certainly difficult to achieve without an enormous expenditure of time and/or money. Even by the middle of the nineteenth century, if survival is any test, there were more patents than commercially viable models. In 1824, Maelzel, who succeeded von Kempelen as proprietor of the Turk, patented a talking doll in Paris; in 1853, Guillard, a Frenchman, patented one made of wood, and a year later Alexandre Theroude improved one of his own earlier designs, creating a doll that could say '*Maman*', '*Papa*' and a bizarre touch straight out of the Black Forest – 'Cou-Cou'. Patents for crying dolls and musical dolls followed, and by the 1860s some of the main technical and financial problems must have been overcome, since makers were regularly producing talking dolls. However, the limitations of the miniaturised bellow-and-pipes system restricted their vocabulary

Left
Walking doll by Steiner. French. 1875. Bethnal Green Museum, London.

Opposite
Talking Doll by Jumeau. (*left*). 1885; and Talking Doll by H. J. Much (*right*). *c.* 1875. Bethnal Green Museum, London.

to '*Maman*', '*Papa*' and, where deemed desirable, 'Cou-Cou'. An early example was a French Steiner doll that spoke, moved her mouth and eyes, and alternated swinging her arms and legs, but although the doll was unable to walk on her own without human aid, Steiner eventually made a virtue of her limitations by advertising her as *Bébé Premier Pas* ('The First Step Doll').

Development continued, and by 1872 Madame Bru, who had succeeded her husband as head of the firm, was taking out a patent for a singing doll. A decade later there were American and German competitors on this line (Webber 1882; Hölbe 1883), and in 1892 Girard's *Bébé Marcheur* combined walking and talking for the first time. By the 1900s this had become a quite common feat.

(The *Bébé Marcheur* may have been a Bru doll, with Girard acting only as the firm's representative.)

All but the last of these developments coincided with the great era of French doll making. The girl-woman and sophisticated girls of Jumeau and Bru were therefore equipped to perform appropriately genteel actions, or, on occasion, to utter

Above
The Singing Doll by Webber. American. Wax head and real hair. Advertised as 'French-made doll' which came in two sizes. A more expensive version of the doll had eyes which closed when the doll was laid down. It also came with a knitted chemise. From an 1880s American magazine advertisement.

Right
Bébé Marcheur, a walking doll with clockwork mechanism and go-cart. By Roullett/Decamps. French. 1892. Height: 30.48 cm (12 in). Warwick Toy Museum.

appropriately filial sentiments. They powdered their noses at dressing tables, blew soap bubbles, pushed little carts about, and, when the pursuit became respectable and fashionable, rode bicycles. These little *fin de siècle* figures even played at being dairy-maids – the traditional gesture of the sophisticate, half in love with rural innocence; perhaps it is not too fanciful to see a sinister parallel in the fact that Queen Marie Antoinette – the leader of another refined, pleasure-loving and doomed society – acted out the same fantasy during regular visits to her dairy at Rambouillet.

The Bru factory showed the strongest penchant for mechanical novelties, putting on the market a range of *bébés* that could be realistically tended by their child 'mothers'. There was a crying doll, a drinking doll, a *Bébé Gourmand* that could be fed sweets (returning them through an opening in her foot), and finally, in 1892 a baby that appeared to breathe as well as talk. Bru, like several other makers, produced a two-faced doll whose head turned to show a smiling or a tearful face,

according to the owner's whim. Other factories were responsible for babies that crawled and cork dolls that swam. The swimming was developed surprisingly early, in 1876 – by a designer named E. Martin. Two years later it was manufactured and distributed, as 'Ondine', by Charles Bertran of Paris. Inside her cork body, Ondine carried a well-protected clockwork movement that worked her limbs in a convincing breast stroke, actually propelling her through the water. Dolls that walked or danced to music (produced by a concealed musical box mechanism) were popular in this and later periods, but perhaps the culmination of nineteenth-century French ingenuity was a kissing doll marketed by the Steiner Company in 1897. This winsome creature, when prompted by the pull of a cord, would say 'Mama' or 'Papa' and then move its lips to kiss whoever was holding it, and, when put to bed, the doll could be induced to wail, presumably in protest, just like a child.

Interesting dolls were also made in the United States before 1860, including some fine hand-

carved examples, traditional corn dolls and original rag dolls, but they were essentially parochial and, in any case, non-mechanical. Until late in the nineteenth century, larger numbers of dolls were imported from Germany, and perhaps as many quality dolls' heads, which American makers would then provide with a body – with the result that bodies rather than dolls were the frequent subjects of American patent applications. When they wanted luxury dolls, Americans tended to import them from Paris. Their home production generally consisted of figures that retailed for no more than a few dollars, but even so, many were impressively complex, although often too involved with working prams, sewing machines, or rocking cradles to rank as 'proper' dolls in the eyes of purists who often seemed to think that any activity but a gentle stroll was unladylike. However, no such objection was raised to the hyperactive 'creeping baby' invented by Robert J. Clay in 1871. This infant, clothed in the bonnet and dress proscribed by contemporary fashion, alternately moved its hands and feet as it crawled along the floor, occasionally glancing to one side as if to check on the presence of an admiring audience. It was made by several American firms including Ives. Americans also had a distinctive taste for humorous dolls with a contemporary national reference (the Heathen Chinee, the Negro Preacher, Uncle Sam).

As performers, the best American dolls were really little inferior to their French counterparts, but what distinguished them from each other was that while the American dolls reflected life in the household, fields or workshop, the French dolls inhabited a luxurious and leisurely world of rose petals and soap bubbles. No wonder the hard-working American-puritan used to believe that Europe was both sinful and decadent: even

Above
Walking nurserymaid and pram. French. *c.* 1880. Jumeau swivel head. Mechanism by Decamps of Paris. Height: 30.48 cm (12 in). Worthing Museum and Art Gallery.

Right
The Lady with the Lyre. Life-sized breathing musical automaton. By J. Phalibois. International Doll Library Foundation, New York.

Above
A variety of mechanical dolls including (*back left*) French bicycling doll, Blondin, *c*. 1880, height: 20 cm (8 in), and (*front left*) bicycling doll by Althof Bergmann, with Hawkins. American. 1870. Museum of London.

Right
An example of the walking dolls manufactured by J. & E. Stevens and George W. Brown & Co. and others during the 1870s. This doll has one of the mechanisms patented in 1868 by William Goodwin of New York. The mechanism is mounted under the seat of the carriage. The doll's head is made of *papier mâché.* The base is made of cloth. Margaret Woodbury Strong Museum, Rochester.

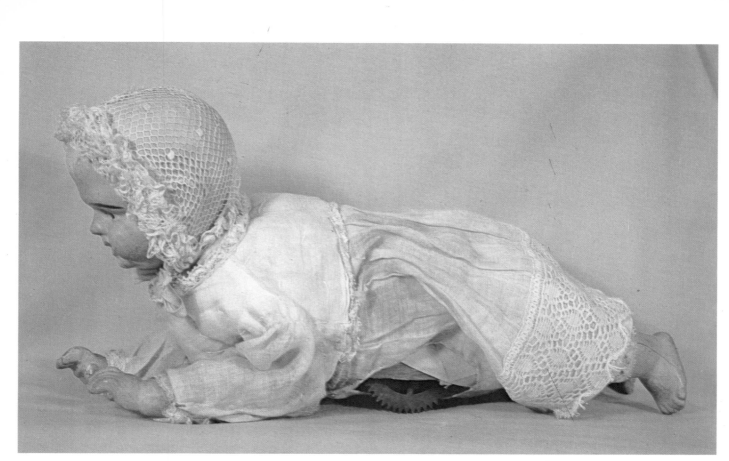

Above
The Creeping Baby patented in 1871 by Robert J. Clay of New York. The doll, whose hands and feet are made of composition, and whose composition body is covered with wax, was manufactured by the Automatic Toy Works of New York 1871-81, and then later by E. R. Ives & Co. of Bridgeport, Connecticut 1882-1900. Margaret Woodbury Strong Museum, Rochester.

Right
The patent paper for Robert J. Clay's Creeping Baby. Margaret Woodbury Strong Museum, Rochester.

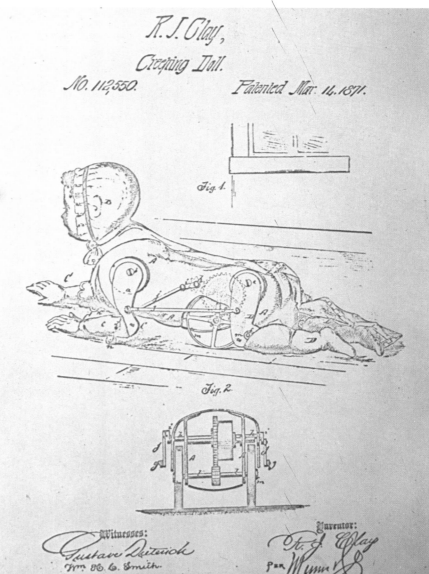

The Snake Dance (original version)
by Jean Roullet. French. 19th cent.
Sotheby's, London.

the non-speaking dolls of the day attested to the fact.

Until the 1880s, the supremacy of Parisian doll-makers was unchallenged, at least as far as the quality trade was concerned, but then the German factories took the lead again, effectively dominating the world market until 1914. Firms such as Simon & Halbig, Handwerck, the Heubach Brothers and Armand Marseille took over the *bébé* from the French and produced it at a much lower price, although they still tended to have their dolls dressed in Paris. One of the effects on the French firms was to promote a series of mergers from 1899 onwards, when Jumeau, Bru and other well-known names disappeared into the Société Francaise de Fabrication des Bébés et Jouets (French Society for the Manufacture of Dolls and Toys), leaving a consequent diminution in variety and individuality. The situation in the later nineteenth century was neatly summed up by Hope Howard, an American, in an 1887 issue of *St Nicholas* magazine:

Now Germany is really the Doll Country. We are told of the Paris doll as the representative of 'its race'. It is true that the doll population of France and especially of Paris is very large; but it is essentially a class race in the latter place. As you pass through the streets you see them dressed in the latest mode and looking at you out of their great eyes for approval of their style. But in Dresden and other German cities, you see dolls of every rank. You see them in every style of dress and undress. You encounter them in every nationality represented by its peculiar costume . . .

84

The German makers created novelties too (the drinking doll), and they achieved some technical advances that made for greater realism: dolls' eyelids, previously moved by the primitive method of pulling a wire attached to the body, from the 1880s were worked by lead counter-weights so that the doll 'slept' and 'woke up' convincingly; and from 1906, dolls' eyeballs could be made to move from side to side. But the decisive advance in talking devices for dolls was in fact to be the work of an American: the famous inventor Thomas Alva Edison. In 1877, he stumbled on the technique for making a machine to record and reproduce the voice. His discovery – the phonograph – was the accidental result of his efforts to record telephone messages; and the Phonographic Doll, patented by Edison in 1878, although not commercially or technically feasible until 1889, when production began at a factory set up by Edison, was therefore the by-product of a by-product.

The Edison doll was first publicly seen at the Paris Exhibition of 1890, and shortly afterwards at the Lennox Lyceum in New York City, where a dozen of the dolls were lined up, each in turn reciting a verse from 'Mother Goose'. The doll was exactly what her name suggested: a little figure containing a small phonograph which enabled her to recite the nursery rhymes. The phonograph was started by a little winder attached to the doll's waist. The body, made of steel, was manufactured in the United States, but the head was German bisque, made by the firm of Simon & Halbig. *The Scientific American* of 26 April 1890 described how the recordings were made for Edison's doll:

The wax-like records are placed upon an instrument very much like an ordinary phonograph, in the mouth of which a girl speaks the words to be repeated by the doll. A number of these girls are continually doing this work. Each one has a

stall to herself, and the jangle produced by a number of girls simultaneously repeating 'Mary had a little lamb', 'Jack and Jill', 'Little Bo-peep', and other interesting stories is beyond description. These sounds united with the sounds of the phonographs themselves when reproducing the stories make a veritable pandemonium.

Left
Kissing doll with glass sleeping eyes, which walks, talks, turns its head, and throws kisses with its hands. French. 1905. Height: 49.53 cm (19 in). Bethnal Green Museum, London.

Below
American clockwork walking doll with painted cast-metal head and boots. The doll can move backwards and forwards by means of wooden rollers concealed inside the boots. Manufactured by Ives & Co., of New York *c*. 1880. Height: 24 cm (9.6 in). Christie's, London.

In doll terms, the significance of the advance was that artificially produced speech had been replaced by artificially *re-*produced speech. This was a much bigger step than the one, made after the Second World War, from phonographs to

Walking, talking doll with eyes that open and close. By Simon & Halbig. German. *c.* 1910. Museum of London.

transistors and tape recorders. The Edison factory is said to have been able to make five hundred phonograph dolls a day, but, if so, it can hardly have worked at capacity for very long. Since Edison dolls are extremely rare, it seems unlikely that many were made – especially as they retailed at twenty dollars apiece. That, at any rate, was the claim by *The Doll's Dressmaker* in 1891, when the magazine offered an Edison

Talking Doll to the girl who collected the largest number of subscribers for the magazine.

Like so many pioneering inventions, Edison's was too expensive to be commercially satisfactory, and others reaped the harvest he had sown. Despite his patents, Edison was faced with competitors in his own country as well as in Europe (Arnold, Lambert, etc). The most notable was Jumeau's *Bébé Phonographe* of 1893, advertised as a talking and singing doll that had a vocabulary of seventy-five words, and depending on the phonographic cylinder used, could speak in French, English and Spanish. (Like most milestones this has been surpassed in modern times: an Italian doll named Lilly 'speaks' nine languages). Ambitious talking dolls enjoyed great popularity until the 1920s, when the novelty wore off. It is tempting to suppose that children really prefer silent dolls whose speech can be created by the owner's imagination but, on the other hand, it is undeniable that dolls leaving almost nothing to the imagination are among the greatest commercial successes of the last twenty years.

Until quite recent times the overwhelming majority of Western dolls have been girls. Baby dolls have been reasonably common since their introduction in the nineteenth century; boy dolls much less so; and convincing representations of adults and old people rare indeed except for portrait dolls or caricatures. One part of the explanation may be that the little girl doll can be adapted to several roles – the real little girl's 'child', or her friend, or even herself in Toyland. Boys, of course, were not supposed to be interested in dolls. Rougher, more 'manly' play was expected of them, hence the masses of expendable tin soldiers rather than the individual fragile doll; the soldier-doll is not unknown, but he usually turns out to be an adult toy – a souvenir, or a portrayal of a famous general (such

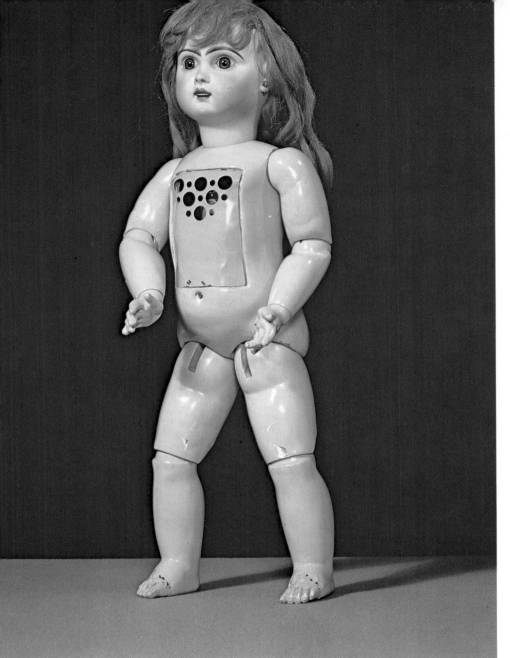

Roosevelt – enthusiastic marksman though he was – drew the line at killing such a small, helpless animal, and the journalists made as much as they could of the story. Cartoonist Clifford Berryman took the story a stage further, combining the boundary and the bear cub ideas in a scene labelled 'Drawing the Line in Mississippi', which was syndicated all over the United States. This in turn inspired Morris Mitchom, a New York toy-shop owner, to start making and selling plush-covered bears, each displayed in his shop window as 'Teddy's Bear', alongside a copy of Berryman's drawing. Some soft toys, mechanical and otherwise, had been manufactured previously, but the bear had never established itself as any kind of children's favourite; now, however,

Left
Jumeau's *Bébé Phonographe*. French. 1890. Bethnal Green Museum, London.

Below
Teddy Roosevelt doll manufactured in 1909 by Albert Schoenhut of Philadelphia. The jointed wooden figure is held together with cloth-covered elastic cords. Margaret Woodbury Strong Museum, Rochester.

as Lord Kitchener). Real boy's dolls appeared surprisingly late in the day: the Golliwog after about 1890, after it was featured in a series of children's books; and the Teddy Bear after 1903 as a shrewd exploitation of a hunting incident in the career of President Theodore ('Teddy') Roosevelt. In November 1902, 'Teddy' Roosevelt had visited Mississippi in order to arbitrate a boundary dispute between that state and Louisiana. This was not a particularly exciting subject for the journalists, who were included to manufacture some 'silly season' news out of the president's hunting activities, but when a bear cub wandered into his sights,

Right
Thomas Edison's Phonograph Doll as featured in the *Scientific American* in 1890.

Below
Clockwork walking doll with painted cast-metal heads and boots. The doll can move backwards and forwards by means of six wooden rollers concealed inside the boots. American. Patented 1875. Height: 24 cm (9.6 in). Sotheby's, London.

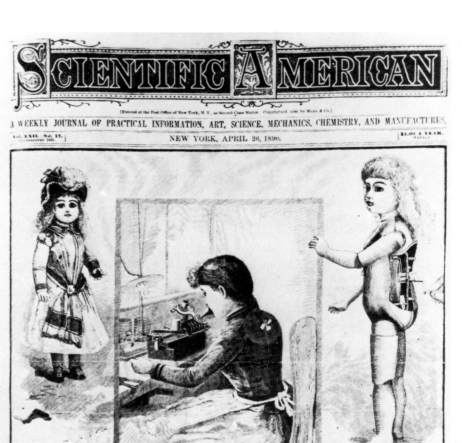

Debut of Edison's Talking Doll as featured by the Scientific American in 1890. The processes of recording her songs and other manufacturing steps are shown.

Mitchom did well enough to put his new line on a more legitimate footing. With the politeness of those far-off days he wrote to 'T. R.' asking whether the president would allow the use of his name. 'I don't think my name is likely to be worth much in the bear business, but you are welcome to use it', was Teddy's reply. With a slight adjustment, they have remained 'Teddy's Bears' ever since. But although Mitchom named them, he did not start the great Teddy Bear craze. That was caused by the toy bears of Margarete Stieff, a German, which were imported into the United States in 1905–6 and then copied or made with variations everywhere. Afterwards, bears of all sizes, types, and nationalities sold in huge quantities for several years. Among the multitude of contemporary advertisements are 'self-whistling' bears, tumbling bears, the brain child of the Fast Black Skirt Company, and 'Electric Bright Eye Teddy Bears – shake the right paw, eyes light up – white or red'. Unlike most nursery crazes, Teddy Bears survived the end of the first excitement, and have enjoyed unbroken popularity ever since. As early as 1907 the Sears, Roebuck catalogue advertisement was calling them The Best Plaything Ever Invented, 'Not a fad or a campaign article, but something which has come to stay on merit alone'. And so it proved.

Imitations of the Adult World

Mothers and fathers, doctors and nurses, cops and robbers – children spend a good deal of their play time directly imitating the way adults behave, and assuming adult roles with intense seriousness. This is generally believed to be a valuable part of growing up; it helps to make children into co-operative social beings and makes them familiar with the gestures and manoeuvres adults use to cope with realities.

The mimicry may be direct or indirect, depending on whether the player identifies with an adult role or merely projects the role on to a toy. Almost all the toys considered so far relate to this last kind of play. The more direct kind of mimicry, that which often involves other children or their toy substitutes, does not necessarily require the presence of toys at all, the substantial act of imagination being enough. But children like to have the most realistic accessories they can get to support their imagination, and the ever increasing number of mechanical objects in everyday life is paralleled by the ever-increasing number of their toy equivalents.

For many children the kitchen is the vital centre of the home, just as the stomach is the vital centre of the nervous system, and toy utensils, cutlery and other impedimenta have a long history. In the nineteenth century,

Above
Left: A German housemaid chasing a mouse with her broom. Possibly by Guntermann. *c.* 1900. *Right:* Lehmann's Tyrus. 1900-14. Private collection.

Left
Toy stove and accessories as displayed in the *Au Bon Marché* catalogue of 1907.

Above Left
An electro-static machine and accessories for 'electric experiences' and Marconi's telegraph. Available in several models: with bell, with receiver, or with clockwork movement. From *Au Bon Marché*'s 1907 catalogue.

Above Right
Sewing machine doll by Sandt. German. 1892. Height: 19 cm (7.5 in). Estrid Faurhold collection.

Opposite
Right: Bizzie Lizzie, a German housemaid. *c.* 1925. *Left:* A German flower-seller. *c.* 1910. Strangers' Hall Museum, Norwich.

Below
A box of accessories for 'electric, instructive, and amusing' experiences. From *Au Bon Marché*'s 1907 catalogue.

working toy cookers were widely advertised. The Dainty Toy Range came for as little as fifty cents, 'nickel-plated with polished edges and (high Victorian) ornamentation', with a few utensils thrown in for good measure. The toy heating stove was equally ornate, though more foursquare and upright in appearance; a lighted candle was placed inside, and its flame, seen through translucent red windows, adequately simulated burning fuel.

There were home-made toy stoves, too. In Louisa May Alcott's *Little Men*, Jo makes her niece Daisy a doll's kitchen, including:

a cooking stove. Not a tin one, that was of no use, but a real iron stove, big enough to cook for a large family of very hungry dolls. But the best of it was that a real fire burned in it, real steam came out of the nose of the little tea-kettle, and the lid of the little boiler actually danced a jig, the water inside bubbled so hard.

After the cooking, the cleaning: washing machines, clothes wringers and carpet sweepers were all on sale before 1900. The toy wringer appeared in the United States through sheer accident. The Triumph Wringer Company of Keene, New Hampshire, made a model wringer as an advertising gimmick – only to find that the model was more popular than their product. With admirable realism, the firm switched to making toy wringers. The number of these miniature domestic items that originated or became popular in the United States is quite striking, and may well reflect a real difference between American and European society – or at least between those Americans and Europeans who could afford this kind of toy. As with mechanical dolls and other toys the American nineteenth-century outlook – created by settlement and expansion – made for lively, homely, humorous toys that made an interesting contrast with the refined whimsicalities of the European tradition. In Europe, gentility was associated absolutely with freedom from manual labour: a lady might supervise the cook or housekeeper, or might pour the tea, but had no direct contact with kitchen utensils or cleaning

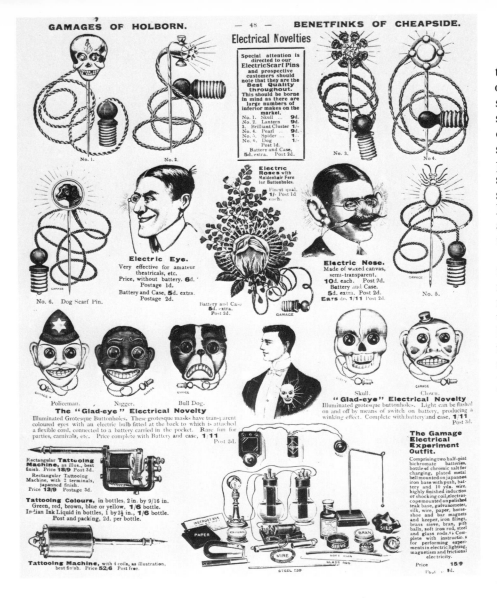

tools. America, still in the process of being settled, was at least superficially more egalitarian in spirit, and certainly less caste-conscious. Apart from east coast socialites, even quite comfortably placed American women with servants were not adverse to spending some time in the kitchen; and the difference in attitude is as apparent in toys as in the literature of the time.

After the cooking and cleaning, there came the making and mending of clothes. Some miniature sewing machine models were not intended as toys at all, but as convenient adult portables for minor tasks, although toy sewing machines were made as well, for instance, the Triumph Toy Sewing Machine:

A first class machine that will sew perfectly. It has the latest patent feed motion, a perfect stitch regulator, uses the Wilcox & Gibbs self setting needle which has a short blade and long shank and is not easily broken. On account of the simple device embodied in its construction it runs lighter and quicker than any machine made. It is fastened to the table with a clamp

Above
A page from Gamage's 1913 Christmas Bazaar catalogue showing the newest electrical novelties, including two tattooing machines.

Right
The Bingophone, a child's gramophone made by Bing of Nuremberg. *c.* 1925. Sotheby's, London.

furnished with each machine. Elegantly enamelled and finished in flower designs. Suitable for the little miss, for the nursery maid, for all kinds of plain family sewing and is adapted largely for kindergarten use. Boxed, with a sample and spare needle, $1.25 in 1902. Why bother with the real thing?

After the washing, wringing, and mending, the pressing: one type of ordinary domestic iron (also called, more picturesquely, a sad iron) could be heated by lifting its hinged lid and putting in a hot coal; smaller versions made for children are known from very early in the nineteenth century.

An even more fearsome accessory for Doctors and Nurses was the 'Novelty Medical Coil and Battery complete' advertised by Montgomery Ward:

This battery is especially designed for amusement purposes, but when required will serve the purposes of the best medical coils. It is provided with small hand regulator, and currents thus produced range from the mildest to those that are quite enough for the strongest man.

This was not advised as a novelty for adults, but appeared in the toy section of the catalogue, between see-saw chimes and magnets. Fortunately electro-therapy was less widely known in the 1890s, or some excruciating home psychiatry might have been practised with the aid of the medical coil.

Other aspects of the traditionally male working world were equally well represented in small ploughs, wheelbarrows, tools, and so on, but apart from steam engines, its mechanical side was less in evidence, although Ward did advertise a toy lawnmower which really worked.

By the time toy typewriters had appeared, at the end of the century, typing had become an almost exclusively female occupation, providing opportunities for large numbers of the better educated young women to escape from home life and the instant marriage market; and thus, with bicycling and office jobs, made possible the phenomenon of the emancipated 'New Woman', as controversial in her day as the Woman's Libber is now. The typewriter was an expensive toy with a limited middle-class market. In the United States, McLoughlin's Young People's Typewriter retailed for five dollars during the early years of the twentieth century; the advertising claiming that the machine was comparable in quality to the expensive adult models. In Britain, all the Army and Navy Store's catalogues up until the 1930s feature only one model, the Simplex, which was not even a true typewriter but roughly resembled a Dymo – with a disc that had to be dialed to print each letter. This did, however, make it relatively cheap: the inflation-conditioned mind boggles at the virtually unchanged price of about five shillings (25p) charged for this basic model between 1907 and 1926. Since then, the typewriter has never been a really satisfactory toy. If it is to be at all efficient, it must be too close to the real thing (and too expensive as a toy) to justify its existence; and if inefficient, like so many modern plastic models, it breaks or jams more easily than is acceptable in a toy that is still by no means cheap.

Right
Bingola I, a child's tinplate gramophone which came with operating instructions in six languages. Made by Bing of Nuremberg. *c.* 1920. Sotheby's, London.

Below
The Hartford Rocker. From an 1880s American advertisement.

MERRY CHRISTMAS!

"THE HARTFORD ROCKER,"
GRISWOLD'S PATENT.
Amuses one, two or three for hours; commended by physicians and mothers; develops chest and limbs; is light, durable and handsome; cannot be upset; a lasting gift. Sent on receipt of price $8, or C. O. D.
HARTFORD ROCKER CO., Hartford, Conn.

The same sort of objections apply to record players, still cameras, movie cameras, and also television sets, apart from the plastic nursery versions that are actually just slide shows put on inside a box; in recent years, however, some of these have been able to produce some quite sophisticated effects.

The toy telephone makes an eminently satisfactory plaything, even in an entirely non-mechanical version, since the invented dialogue is the most important element in a child's play. However, telephones with bell attachments were manufactured early on by bell specialists such as the Gong Bell Company, and various refinements, such as an answering voice, have been featured from time to time. Before the Second World War, Gong Bell even anticipated the videophone with

their Television Playphone, on which the 'caller' could turn on pictures representing the people he was supposed to be calling. Nowadays, of course, the working toy telephone and walkie-talkie are quite common.

Most new forms of transport have been copied or adapted as toys with remarkable speed; and not only as toys to push around or set in motion, but as small versions of the real thing which a child could get onto or into as well as operate.
Little carts drawn by dogs or sheep were known for centuries as luxury toys only; but from medieval times the ordinary child happily pranced about astride a hobby-horse, which consisted of a long stick with an imitation horse's head stuck on it. By the time bicycles developed, in the nineteenth century, children were able to have toys far closer to the

Above
A child's sewing machine (late 19th cent.) and typewriter (c. 1935). Both German. Bethnal Green Museum, London.

Opposite Top
Pixiephone. Bethnal Green Museum, London.

Opposite Bottom
A doll's tea party automaton. c. 1900. Castle Museum, York.

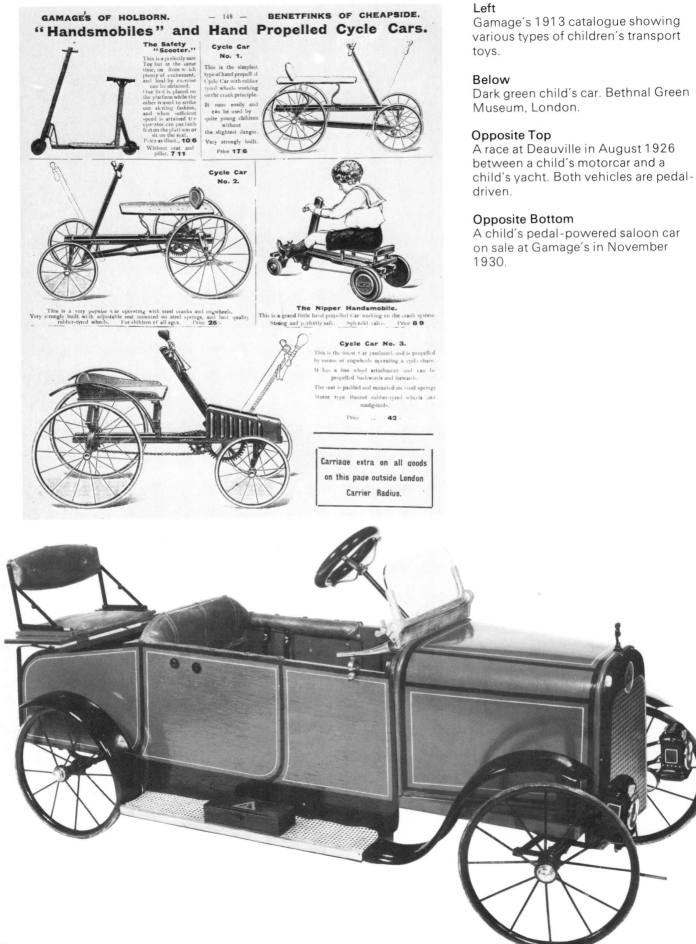

Left
Gamage's 1913 catalogue showing various types of children's transport toys.

Below
Dark green child's car. Bethnal Green Museum, London.

Opposite Top
A race at Deauville in August 1926 between a child's motorcar and a child's yacht. Both vehicles are pedal-driven.

Opposite Bottom
A child's pedal-powered saloon car on sale at Gamage's in November 1930.

originals. In fact, many early versions of the bicycle (or tricycle) were so impractical that they had novelty value only, and appealed to children more than to adults. The Draisine, for example, invented in 1816–17 by Baron Karl von Drais, was hardly more than a hobby horse fitted with wheels; indeed the British nicknamed it the 'dandy horse'. It operated on the scooter principle: the 'cyclist' ran along on the tips of his toes until he had acquired sufficient momentum to lift his feet from the ground and let the wheels carry him along for a while. A few years later, machines that could be driven manually were made: the operator pulled and pushed two levers attached to the back axle, while steering with his two feet on the front axle. One American firm, advertising a three-wheeler version for children in the 1850s, made much of the arm and chest muscles that this 'propeller' would develop.

When females did take to the bicycle, around 1890, it was to comfortable, pneumatic-tyred, chain-linked pedal bikes that made it worth braving the abuse of the outraged males. In the meantime (the 1860s), Pierre Lallement had conceived of the idea of foot-pedals, which he then developed to attach to the front-wheel axle, thus making possible an instrument that was of some practical value but (by all accounts) sheer agony to use: the steel-wheeled 'boneshaker'. The inventions that went to create the pneumatic-tyred 'safety bicycle' of modern times were made in the 1880s; and it was only after this that cycling became a mass amusement for adults and children alike.

The bicycle is only partly a toy. Except when used for racing, it is ridden less for amusement than for speedy transportation. Tricycles, on the other hand, are toys in the full sense, since they create an illusion of travelling that is more important than the actual distance covered. Adult tricycles were quite popular in the 1880s

Above
A bright red Austin child's car made in
the 1950s. Bethnal Green Museum,
London.

Right
A child's cream and scarlet two-seater
model limousine. Made entirely of
wood, it is carefully sprung, has
luggage space, spring steel bumpers,
sliding windows on the door and a
sunroof. Its one-half horse-power
electric motor, with batteries capable
of 32 km (20 miles) to a charge, can
reach a speed of 8-11.2 km (5-7 m)
per hour. 1938.

and 1890s, and for some time
afterwards they continued to be
used commercially for light
deliveries. But in this century they
have been produced almost
exclusively for small children, for
whom the 'trike' – so much more
stable than the 'bike' – offers
obvious advantages. An
interesting example of changing
social attitudes can be seen in the
career of the horse tricycles a
tricycle with a horse's head and
neck attached to the handlebars,
so that the child could pretend he
or she was galloping along rather
than cycling; much the same
arrangement occurred on the old
manually 'pedalled' tricycle

discussed earlier. Presumably this
signified that horse-riding was a
normal, socially prestigious, or
perhaps a nostalgic occupation.
The horse tricycle was still being
sold in the years before the First
World War, but it then
disappeared – which might have
signified acceptance of the
complete transition to a wholly
human-controlled means of
transportation, and the demise of
the horse as a part of everyday
life.

A rather strange clockwork-toy
variation on the horse-tricycle is a
machine with a doll in the saddle,
on display at the Museum of
Childhood in Edinburgh. The

doll 'drives' with long ribbon-
reins that lead to a bird, perched
on the handlebars, which is
apparently pulling the
contraption – an imaginary
peacock-cum-paradise bird with
multi-coloured feather wings and
a gold-spangled body.

The use of the pedal principle
in other forms of toy transport is
well known. The most enduringly
popular has been the pedal car,
which appeared on the market as
early as 1904–5 in the United
States and France. The earliest
models tended to be very
expensive as well as luxurious.
Amongst these custom built
special models were splendid

small versions of the now vintage cars that have so much nostalgic appeal, with their big wheels, gleaming bodywork and big bulbous horns. One model even incorporated a rattle device to simulate the noise of an engine. Many of these cars were actually made by automobile firms such as Studebaker, Renault and, apparently, in lovingly accurate detail, by the Bugatti racing car factory. A few years later, British department stores were selling pedal cars on the normal first-come-first-served basis, but the price was still terribly high – in the region of £2 10s (£2.50) at a time when 25 per cent of British men earned less than half that amount for a week's work. (Women, of course, earned far less than men in those days). For the most part, fire engines and locomotives, which aroused quite some enthusiasm, belong to a later period when pedal toys were being produced more cheaply, but pedal versions of ships and aeroplanes seem never to have developed much of a following; they are presumably too far removed from reality to allow a willing suspension of childish disbelief.

Nowadays, recruiting advertisements tend to make military service sound like a craft apprenticeship with full board – certainly nothing much to do with pulling a trigger. But for most of history it was quite otherwise: valour and the military arts were valued for what they were, and prized more highly than almost anything else. War was 'the sport of kings', and royal children were encouraged to master its techniques as early as possible. As a small child, Louis XIV of France was presented with a complete army of silver and gold soldiers made by a goldsmith from Nancy – not just the musketeers and gunners who would appeal to the ordinary boy, but specialist troops such as the pioneers who fortified or undermined citadels. Whatever the firepower of Louis's little gold cannon, they were still

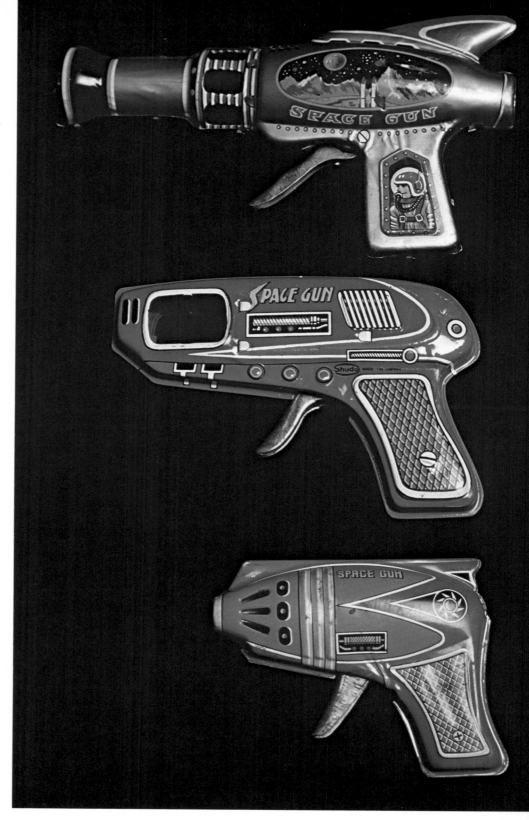

drawn by non-mechanical energy – in this case by a team of fleas. A little later, when he was nine, the chief minister, Cardinal Mazarin, gave Louis a miniature fort defended by guns that actually fired blanks. With or without Louis's connivance, the blanks caught fire and exploded; and for a few years his training in the

Friction-driven space guns which make sparks when shot. *Left to right:* 10, 14, and 19 cm (4, 5, 6, and 7.6 in) long. All Japanese. Private collection.

military arts was conducted on less determindly realistic lines.

In the late nineteenth century a little brass cannon was an acceptable plaything in Russia, if we can believe Dostoyevski's *Brothers Karamazov*. In a characteristically frantic scene, the boy owner, Kolya Krasotkin, brings the gun along to entertain a dying friend and his family with a satisfying flash-bang display, although for this occasion he puts up with the use of powder – but no small shot – as a concession to the indoor nature of the show. In the United States, too, children were still quite likely to be handling real weapons, since frontier traditions – and, in some areas, frontier conditions – were still strong. But for most city boys, in America as in Europe, the use of gunpowder was controlled by its being measured out into tiny quantities known as caps. An exception was the large toy/model warship, which was sometimes equipped with guns that worked with gunpowder and shot; German examples with delayed-action devices were tremendously impressive in operation, as well as – relatively – safe.

Top

A page from Gamage's 1913 catalogue advertising children's pedal-operated toy motorcars of which there were 'hundreds in stock'. All of these models feature speedometer, horn, clock, lamps, brake, but come also offered with pneumatic tyres and pump (*top right and bottom left*) or adjustable seat (*middle right*).

Above

A page from Gamage's 1913 catalogue showing various 'harmless' toy pistols and cannons. These were designed to fire either peas or small leaden bullets (*second from top left*), peas and rubber balls (*second row from top, centre*), or rubber shells and caps (*middle row left and centre and second row from bottom left and right*).

Cap guns have always been popular since they combine a simple, reliable mechanism with a noisy and realistic effect. The cap bomb – basically a metal sandwich with a cap filling – is more suitable for practical jokes, since it can be dropped from a height, generally with the intention of missing the victim and going off on impact with the floor. The most curious of cap pistols, were those made out of iron in the nineteenth century by J. & E. Stevens and other American firms. Some of these represented animal figures, such as a sea serpent which exploded a cap by snapping its jaws shut, and the monkey which hammered a cap with a coconut; others were political and tropical, like Ives's The Chinese Must Go pistol, the trigger of which was a Chinaman's pigtail.

Other types of toy gun are legion. Merely to survey the field is to realise how much more ingenuity has gone into mimic death-dealing than into any other toys mentioned in this chapter – not a reassuring thought in view of the importance of role-playing for the future adult. Quite apart from the static models that only click, there have been noise-makers like the sub-machine guns that operate on the principle of dragging a toothed wheel round so that every tooth strikes a bar; light-makers such as the battery-operated laser gun and some older, more ingenious guns that actually smoked after being fired; spring guns that shoot hard peas, marbles, rubber balls, and wooden sticks with suction caps on the ends; water pistols and potato guns, worked by air pressure; and the pop-gun's older brother, developed from the same compressed-air principle – the fear-inspiring air gun, which, however, seems to have caused miraculously few serious accidents.

Musical Toys and Automata

According to documentary evidence singing birds were the first musical automata and it is certainly likely that such a difficult art would begin with the limited and repeated notes of bird song. Early designs for mechanical birds have been attributed to Alexandrian scholar-engineers of the third century B.C., but the incorporation of musical capacity did not occur until many centuries later. In the tenth century A.D. Bishop Liutprand of Cremona, a western ambassador, described the Byzantine Emperor's throne as being placed beside a gilded tree on which mechanical singing birds were perched, but other sources attribute the work to the artificer Leo the Mathematician. In any case, tangible documentary evidence of such spectacular works is rare for not only the tenth century, but also for all other centuries up to the eighteenth.

What really paved the way for the proliferation of musical toys were the eighteenth-century developments of the miniature clockwork movement and the Black Forest cuckoo-clock. These gave rise to an enormous variety of small, highly decorated, and high-quality moving and singing birds that performed in and on all kinds of watches, boxes, jewel cases and stands – and, above all, in quantities of snuff boxes, with

Johnny the Dunce musical automaton. French. 1860. Bethnal Green Museum, London.

beautiful and elaborate cases
some of which were made of gold
and jewels. The singing birds, no
more than one or two centimetres
long, worked by an ingenious
arrangement of steel rods and
levers that moved their wings and
tails, and often their heads, necks
and even eyes; some actually
hopped from one metal branch to
another.

Jaquet-Droz, who was one of
the pioneers in this area, his son,
Henri-Louis, Henri Maillardet,
and other Swiss families (notably
the Bruguiers and Rochats)
became the leaders of a Franco-
Swiss industry producing large
numbers of these and larger
objects, mechanically as well as
artistically of the highest
standard. (France's reputation as
the home of luxury toys, extended
to the mechanical singing bird,
but even great firms like Bontems
of Paris, who worked for the Tsar,
provided only the luxury and the
ingenuity rather than the
specialised craftsmanship: the

movements of their toys were all
imported from Switzerland.)

Life-sized singing birds also
remained popular through the
eighteenth and nineteenth
centuries, although they were
technically simpler to make than
miniature versions. The base of
the life-sized bird's cage concealed
a bird-organ with a bellows
movement: the turning of the
handle passed compressed air
through the pipes to give an
imitation of the bird's song. Often
there was a clock attached, as in
the canary-and-cage made for
Marie Antoinette by the Parisian
maker Robert Robin (1742–99).
Singing birds played their part in
Cox's exhibition at the Spring
Gardens, and Robert-Houdin
featured them in his
performances. One of the first
novelties was made by Louis
Rochat, yet another Swiss master.
This was the singing-bird pistol, a
bejewelled gold object that
'fired' a tiny bird,
simultaneously starting the

Above

Jumeau life-sized smoking automaton and life-sized singing birds in gilt birdcages. The velvet covered base of the smoking automaton contains a bellows mechanism which activates the smoking action, as well as a small cylindrical musical movement. Last quarter 19th cent. Height: 60.96 cm (24 in). The birdcage at the left has a coin-operated mechanism with a coin drawer in its base. French. Late 19th cent. Height: 55.88 cm (22 in). The birdcage at the right is a rare example from Bontems. The octagonal gilt base is inset with eight Sèvres placques depicting various rural pursuits. French. Third quarter of the 19th cent. Height: 48.26 cm (19 in). Sotheby's, London.

Right

Musical box with automaton performing monkeys. The music is produced by a bellows movement in the base. Probably French. c. 1875. Height: 58.42 cm (23 in). Bethnal Green Museum, London.

Simple marotte. The musical box, hidden beneath the dress, is activated by turning the baton. Probably French. Height: 30.48 cm (12 in). Private collection.

musical movement in the butt.

Although relatively numerous, these birds, large and small, were all hand-made luxury items, and remained so throughout the nineteenth century. Cheaper singing-bird boxes appeared only in the twentieth century, when German makers began to use mass-produced parts. Their vogue lasted only a few decades, no doubt because the phonograph was destroying the novelty effect of most musical automata except for the simplest nursery items. One such was an Edwardian penny toy that is far removed from its luxury ancestor. It consists of a crude little bird standing on a bird-box; twisting its pedestal rubs two hardwoods together to produce a fairly convincing twittering sound.

Much more sophisticated musically, though not always so exciting to look at, are the multitude of musical boxes and other items. In these, the clockwork movement drives a cylinder or disc with pins that 'play' the tuned teeth of a steel comb. The first musical box movements seem to have been made around 1770 by a Swiss watchmaker named Favre; if, as is sometimes claimed, earlier examples existed in other places, they failed to 'take' and had no immediate successors. Favre, who worked in Geneva, pioneered an industry which was to grow steadily in expertise and popularity, and become dominated by the Swiss until the 1880s. As with singing birds, most French and German firms who hoped to cash in on musical novelties imported the movements from Switzerland until at least the middle of the nineteenth century. The early products were all miniatures, the encasements including watches, keys, seals, fans, umbrella handles and walking-stick tops; or, more conventionally – though still often formed in the shape of a piano or some other instrument – jewellery cases, sewing work-boxes, sealing wax containers, or snuff boxes. In this craft, too, snuff boxes (with or without singing birds) were the most exquisite and expensive objects of all, made of black composition, tortoiseshell, or precious metals. Some of these products also carried exquisite small figures and groups that walked, danced, juggled or performed acrobatic feats to musical accompaniment. These figures included organ-grinders and musicians; circus performers; dancing bears; monkey orchestras and other overdressed animals; and also beautifully attired ladies who evidently belonged to the leisured class. Other dolls did not walk, but stood on plush-covered musical stands and lifted tea cups to their lips or sat at their dressing tables looking in the mirror and carefully powdering their noses.

As a child, Queen Victoria was given a musical box with dancing figures (now in the Museum of London). Such additions were all the more impressive with the improvement of musical quality in the course of the nineteenth century, and with the development of musical boxes which could play half a dozen tunes at a single performance. The French toymaker Fernand Martin manufactured two virtually identical musical boxes in 1901–2. On top of one a male pianist in tails 'played' *God Save the King* to celebrate the accession of King Edward VII to the throne; the other a lady pianist played various French tunes.

Among the many pretty, luxurious French novelties, is the *marotte*. This was essentially a sophisticated version of the cheap (and silent) doll-on-a-stick called a *poupard*, a doll's head with a musical box beneath it, concealed by a large collar; head and box were mounted on a stick, which had to be whirled round like a baton to set the music going. A few *marottes* were not heads but fully dressed figures with complete torsos and limbs. These were equally charming as dolls, but their overall visual effect was not especially pleasing – one could not help noticing the wooden

Above
The Musician. Life-sized automaton by Jaquet-Droz. Musée d'Art et d'Histoire, Neuchâtel.

stake in the nether regions – but
there were also a few examples,
entirely sound in limb, that stood
on a draped pedestal containing
the movement.

Of all the mechanical figures
associated with music, the finest is
undoubtedly Pierre Jaquet-
Droz's lady Musician, the largest
of the three life-sized automata for
which Jaquet-Droz became
famous. In this piece, a woman
sits at what is called a 'clavecin'
(harpsichord), although in this
case the instrument is actually a
type of keyboard organ. Her
bosom heaves as she leans over the
keyboard (worked by a bellows
movement) and her fingers press
the keys, actually playing the
instrument. At the end of her
performance she bows gracefully
to right and left.

Musical boxes intended as true
children's toys first appeared on
the market as early as 1835 as
generally straightforward metal
boxes with movements much
simplified in the interests of

cheapness; instead of being
spring-driven, they had to be
worked by a hand crank. Such
musical boxes have been made
ever since, basically unchanged
apart from some mechanical
improvements. The type of
musical box most popular with
children has tended to dramatize
the simple box, either presenting
it as a piano the child can pretend
to play; as a barrel organ; or as

some kind of scene, perhaps with
moving figures. One delightful
item that combined play, thrift,
and culture in characteristic
Victorian fashion was a musical
money-box which played
whenever a coin was inserted in
the slot.

As far as nineteenth-century
musical toys were concerned,
Americans were generally content
to import the goods they wanted

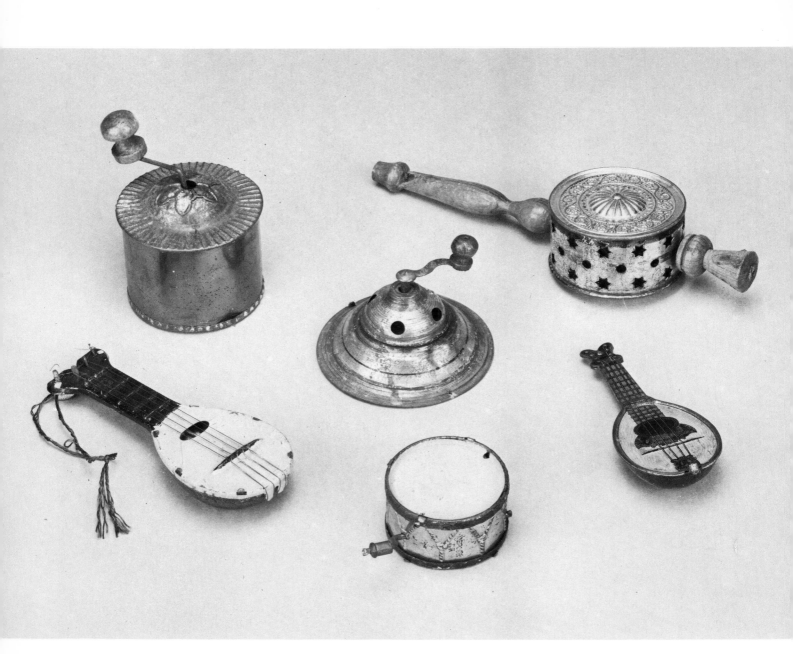

Penny toy musical instruments.
Museum of London.

from Europe, although there were a few noteworthy United States manufacturers. Jerome B. Secor, who was involved with the Ives company, made mechanical singing birds in cages with musical box bases, and also invented a successful whistling bird, marketed by Ives as The American Songster. This was operated by an ingenious tube-and-bulb-with-water device. Secor also made a mechanical piano player and other figures linked with musical movements.

A now well-known company, Milton Bradley, made a musical toy called the Carillion, an automatic musical box in which the hammers of a metalophone (a steel-plated instrument similar to a glockenspiel) are operated by the passage of a Keyboard through the machine by the turning of a crank.

Some of the American mechanical banks were musical, like 'the Dancing Bear Bank with clock-work mechanism and chimes . . . [representing] the front of a country house with an Italian organgrinder and a bear on the lawn'. Instructions for operating the bank were to, 'wind up the mechanism, place a coin in the slot and push the knob', so that the organ-grinder would then 'deposit the coin and play the organ while the bear performs his part'.

As late as 1895, the
Montgomery Ward & Co.
catalogue makes a boast of the
fact that, 'We now import our
entire line of music [sic.] boxes,
buying off the leading
manufacturers of Switzerland'.
But just a few lines further down is
listed the Capital Music Box, 'a
new invention of American
manufacture . . . constructed upon
a new principle', etc., a tendency
often visible in the clockwork toys
while pointing out that
momentum and similar toys have
'no spring to get out of order'.

Musical instruments for
children may be either playable
miniature versions of the real
thing, or make-believe shells
concealing musical box
movements, but, except for the
most expensive (usually custom-
made) examples, miniature
pianos, trumpets, violins and
drums are rarely convincing or
pleasant to the sophisticated ear.
Notable exceptions were
instruments made by Albert
Schoenhut, a German immigrant
to the United States. Originally
employed by a toy warehouse in
Philadelphia, Schoenhut
discovered that he could improve
on the German imported toy
pianos he was called on to repair.
They often arrived with shattered
glass parts which Schoenhut
replaced with carefully tuned

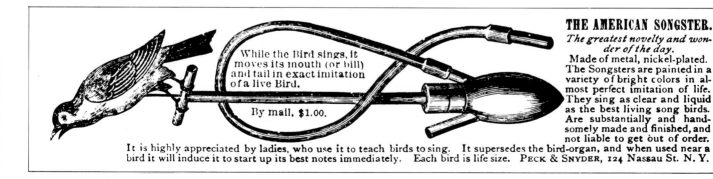

Top
A page from Gamage's 1913
Christmas Bazaar catalogue showing
various types of music boxes.

Above
The American Songster. Invented by
Jerome B. Secor. Manufactured by
Ives & Co. From Gamage's 1913
Christmas Bazaar catalogue.

steel plates. In 1872, he started his own business selling good-quality pianos quite cheaply (about $2 to $12), and gradually built up a substantial enterprise making a range of musical and other toys. However, these achievements were eclipsed after 1900 by the worldwide success of his Humpty-Dumpty Circus. This non-mechanical toy, which consisted of little figures whose jointed and elasticated limbs could be set and kept at all sorts of angles, became one of the most popular toys of all time.

As we have already seen, cheaper toys of all sorts were mass-produced towards the end of the nineteenth century. The expense of incorporating even the most primitive movement put certain limitations on the production of musical toys, but there were plenty of variations on such favourites as the merry-go-round and the organ grinder. American and German musical toys were notable for a greater realism and a more down-to-earth feeling than French makers either looked for or attained. German manufacturers, for example, sold series of whistling men and boys, about thirty centimetres high. These included amiable versions of American, English and Scottish national types, designed to appeal to those markets, although it must be said that the bagpipes produced a sound rather far removed from a whistle. After the 1950s, mass-production of inexpensive musical toys was made possible by a technical innovation that dispensed with the relatively costly Swiss movement: instead of a metal cylinder, a simple, knobbed rubber strip operated the metal prongs.

Small musical boxes are still being manufactured and enjoy a reasonable popularity as luxury goods, novelties, and toys, but larger versions which gave way to

Above
Bristle dolls. Bethnal Green Museum, London.

Opposite
Microphone Sam. American. 1935 Bethnal Green Museum, London.

the record players of the
nineteenth century and
eventually to the jukeboxes of the
twentieth century, have not fared
as well. Originating around 1820,
they quickly surpassed the smaller
boxes in musical quality, owing to
their large movements and
eventual capacity for several
combs with hundreds of teeth. By
the later nineteenth century, firms
such as Nicole-Frères, the leading
makers for most of the nineteenth
century, were producing larger
musical boxes that gave note-
perfect performances of a
convincing range of imitation
orchestral instruments.

From the 1850s to the 1870s,
Wales and McCulloch, the
owners of the Musical Box
Repository of Ludgate Street,
London, were boasting to
Illustrated London News that they
were:

> direct importers of Nicole-Frères
> celebrated Musical Boxes, playing
> with unrivalled brilliancy of tone,
> the best Popular, Operatic and
> Sacred Music. Large sizes, four
> airs, £4 . . . twelve airs £12 12s.
> Snuffboxes, two tunes, 14s 6d and
> 18s . . . four tunes, 40s [£2].

The heyday of the large
musical box began in 1885, when
Lochmann of Leipzig patented his
Symphonion, a musical box in
which the cylinder was replaced
by a disc – the significance of the
innovation being that such a disc
could easily be changed for a new
one with new tunes, making the
Symphonion and its successors the
precursors to modern record
players or tape recorders. In fact,
the smaller versions were wide,
low boxes which opened up to
reveal the disc – in appearance
very similar to the portable record
player of modern times. The
Symphonion soon found a rival in
the Polyphon, a German make
which dominated the industry
until 1879 when the Regina
Music Company, an American
firm founded by Gustav
Brachhausen, an immigrant from
Leipzig, introduced self-changing
disc machines – in effect, jukeboxes. Around the turn of the

Right
Albert Schoenhut's Humpty Dumpty Circus as advertised in Gamage's 1913 Christmas Bazaar catalogue.

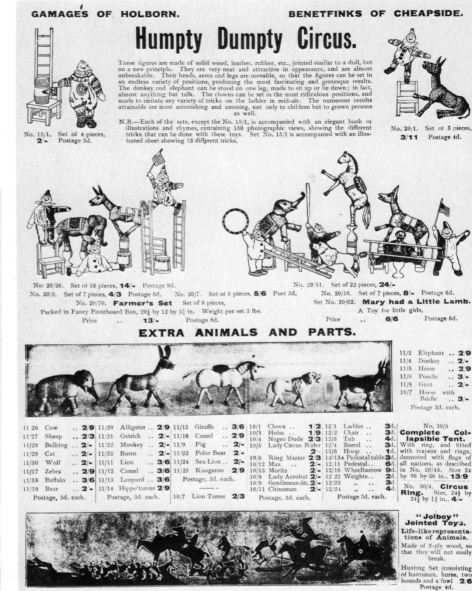

Above
La Parisien, a whistling boy made by Amedée Lafosse in 1892. Canfield collection, Bridgewater.

century, discs were being 'cut' by the thousand and issued every week to cash in on the latest musical hits which, instead of being the operatic airs on the earlier music boxes, were long music-hall programme numbers like 'The Man who Broke the Bank at Monte Carlo'. As penny-in-the-slot machines, Regina Music boxes, with their large balustraded wooden cabinets and high quality of musical reproduction, enjoyed tremendous popularity in fairgrounds, amusement arcades, restaurants, bars, and public houses in the United States and Europe. Thanks to mass-production methods, up until the First World War, even quite poor households had a musical box of one sort or another, but, by that time, the gramophone was starting to become an inexpensive, efficient, and accurate instrument for reproducing sound the popularity of which eclipsed that of the musical box.

One endearing sideline, manufactured since the early days of the gramophone, was an ornament, consisting of a little figure or group which could be attached to the shaft which held the record: when the record turned, the figures danced or performed other actions. Most of these were give-away toys, intended to promote gramophone sales. The idea could be said to derive from the eighteenth-century bristle doll which was essentially a small broom dressed in ordinary clothes (although sometimes these were made of elegantly embroidered silk). When placed on a harpsichord, the doll 'danced' to the vibrations caused by the playing. A recent American equivalent, Microphone Sam, was a tap-dancing Negro who performed similarly.

But the grandest of Victorian toys was the moving musical picture, the rich relative of the penny-in-the-slot machines with their dramas of murder and retribution. The quality Continental tableaux were less horrific but mechanically and musically far superior – splendid three dimensional scenes in which couples danced, windmills whirled and trains rushed about in virtuoso confusion. And all to music!

Left
Polyphon glockenspiel disk musical box. Coin-operated movement. Height: 137 cm (4.56 ft). German. Late 19th cent. Sotheby's, London.

Below
Mechanical picture tableau activated by a clockwork mechanism with three movements. The man in the nightcap and gown tries to strike the mouse. *c.* 1900. 25.5 × 34 cm (10 × 13.5 in). Sotheby's, London.

Optical and Kinetic Toys

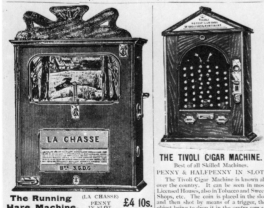

Gamage's catalogue illustrating various types of penny-in-the-slot machines—the early pin-ball and shooting-gallery machines.

For obvious reasons, the theatre as a mechanical amusement has rarely ever matched tableaux of the sort constructed for musical boxes, although these hardly qualify as narratives of conflict and passion.

In true mechanical theatre, the human manager would have to be concealed, but the closest equivalents, such as the performances of Robert-Houdin, were mixed entertainments that no doubt owed a good deal to distracting patter and conjuring skills. Rather more satisfactory from this point of view was a show, put on in the nineteenth century by an American enthusiast, Walter Lindsay of Philadelphia, in which Lindsay's 'mechanical Humpty Dumpty', perched on a stage wall, performed the famous scene from Lewis Carroll's *Through the Looking Glass* with a real little girl acting the part of Alice. By his own account, Lindsay succeeded in capturing on stage the supercilious egomania with which Carroll endowed the old nursery-rhyme character:

(Humpty) gesticulated with his arms, rolled his eyebrows, frowned, turned up his nose in scorn at Alice's ignorance, and smiled from ear to ear when he shook hands with her. Besides this, his mouth kept time with his words all through the dialogue.

Lindsay describes how it was done:

The movement of the mouth, in talking, was produced by a long tape, running down to a pedal, which was controlled by the foot of the performer. And the smile consisted of long strips of red tape, which were drawn out through slits at the corners of the mouth by means of threads which passed through holes in the sides of the head. The performer stood on a box behind the wall, his head just reaching the top of the egg, which was open all the way up the back. At the lower end of the figure, convenient to the hands of the performer, was the row of levers, like a little keyboard; and by striking different chords on the keys, any desired expression could be produced on the face.

Poor Humpty met his end by falling backwards over the wall while somebody behind the scene dropped a box of broken glass, and let the curtain fall.

Other, more self-sufficient dramas took place in the penny-in-the-slot machines of the nineteenth century which presented miniature automata in a stage-like window. These pier and fairground favourites preserved into the twentieth century a popular taste (also reflected in pottery 'fairings') for sensational murders, executions, hauntings, fires, and the serio-comic misfortunes of the drunkard and the married man. A typical example was 'The English Execution': when a coin was put

Above

Minstrel show. The stage encloses a black banjo player sitting in a chair. When the clockwork, housed in a box at the rear of the stage, is wound, banjo music plays and the musician's right forearm simulates playing. Manufactured by Courier Litho. Co. of Buffalo, New York. *c.* 1895. Margaret Woodbury Strong Museum, Rochester.

Left

Living Picture made by Albert Schoenhut. Margaret Whitton collection.

115

into the machine, the gates of the grim prison facade opened to reveal the condemned man at the gallows, with a sacking hood over his head and a rope around his neck. Chimes indicated that the hour of doom has come, while a surpliced priest waved his prayer book up and down. At the ninth chime, the trapdoor opened with sudden violence. The victim fell and the gates closed.

Some *tablaux vivants* – grand ones made in eighteenth-century France, and humbler, more domestic ones made during the nineteenth century – are similar to the scenes created by musical moving pictures of the Victorian era. These include sand pictures and some entertaining clockwork 'Living Pictures' made in the 1870s by Albert Schoenhut's Philadelphia factory. The 'Living Pictures' consisted of movable cardboard cut-outs of heads, arms, etc. which were attached to a fixed background and usually depicted folksy humorous subjects in typical nineteenth-century American style.

So far, performances in which mechanical figures play some part have been discussed, but there were also shows in which the mechanical element is the basis of the entire performance – shows created by a machine or giving the illusion of movement. Where these are playthings, they are generally known as optical and kinetic toys.

The magic lantern, which was invented in the seventeenth century, and which is most often attributed to the Jesuit scientist Athanasius Kircher, although there are disputes over its origin, provided an altogether different and perhaps more seemingly realistic kind of show. First lit by means of a candle, later a paraffin burner, and finally an electric bulb, the lantern was encased in a box with a hole covered by a slide. Light poured through the hole and the slide, and then on through a lens so that the picture was magnified and thrown against a wall or screen.

The English diarist Samuel Pepys saw one demonstrated as early as 1666. On the 19th of August he noted:

But by and by comes by agreement Mr Reeves; and after him Mr Spong; and all day with them . . . upon Opticke enquiries – he (Reeves) bringing me a frame with closes (shutters), on, to see how the rays of light do cut one another, and in a dark room with smoake, which is very pretty. He did also bring lantern with pictures in glass to make strange things appear on a wall, very pretty.

Unfortunately Reeves was an executant rather than a theorist, so Pepys never came to understand how this ancestor of the slide projector worked.

Towards the end of the eighteenth century – that age of festivals, fairs, shows, panoramas and dioramas – the magic lantern became established as a medium for public entertainment. In Paris, the Belgian illusionist E. G. Robertson scored a tremendous success with a show called 'Phantasmagoria', put on in an

Right
Illustration of a magic lantern by Nollet. 1755.

Below
Illustration of a Dubosq Carbon Arc magic lantern.

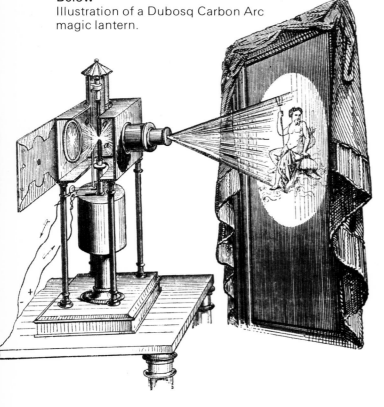

La Lanterne Magique

old monastery. By projecting the picture from behind a muslin screen, the showman kept the magic lantern out of sight, and when ghosts, ghouls and skeletons began to hover threateningly in the night air – with a few additional effects created by distorting lenses and moving shadows – audiences were frightened out of their wits.

Dickens, too, had a yen for terrifying his audience. In *The Cricket on the Hearth*, he conjures up a malevolent child-hating toymaker who:

Had even lost money . . . by setting up Goblin slides for magic lanterns, whereon the Powers of Darkness were depicted as a sort of supernatural shell-fish, with human faces . . . to destroy the peace of mind of any young gentleman between the ages of six and eleven.

By the early nineteenth century, magic lantern shows were quite a common occurrence in the home, and by the second half of the century, when production costs had fallen sufficiently, versions of the magic machine often painted in scarlet and gold or other colour combinations, began to invade the nursery, although it always remained a rather expensive toy.

The usual lanterns had a brass lens holder attached to a tea-caddy body topped with a large-angled Heath-Robinson funnel for the paraffin fumes, but there were a good many examples of Victorian fantasy transforming the magic lantern into something else. One literal-minded manufacturer marketed a model shaped like an actual lantern, another cashed in on a newsworthy event by selling a miniature Eiffel Tower – then

Illustration of a magic lantern from *Histoire des Jouets* by Henri d'Allemagne.

only just completed – with protruding slides and lens-holder.

The slides, too, often beautifully hand painted, are impressive works of art. Most of these were commercially produced, but magic lantern slide-painting kits were put on the market for gifted amateurs. Photographic, transfer-printed and lithographed slides were also manufactured from the late 1850s, offering a variety of moralizing, melodramatic subjects such as the story of 'The Drunkard's Return'. Although the magic lantern was basically a device for showing static subjects, whether in isolation or as part of a sequence, much more sophisticated effects could be achieved. The early 'galantee

117

men', as magic lantern showmen were called, worked with very long slides that could be slowly drawn across the light source to create a kind of narrative, helped out by a clever patter; 'processional' subjects were particularly suitable, for example: Napoleon's army in retreat from Moscow while Cossacks harried them.

In the second half of the nineteenth century, slides with all sorts of special effects were developed, giving fair imitations of movement. Some of these slides were quite substantial objects: one of these generally consisted of a wooden rectangle with a brass-rimmed circular glass – the actual slide – embedded in its centre; the side is either indented or has a lever or crank attached, enabling the operator to produce special effects. But most special effects were produced by enclosing two glass slides within the rectangular frame, one placed over the other: when one of the discs was moved, the picture appeared to change. The simplest form, the slipping slide, was simply a single disc with supplementary pieces that could be pulled into position by tabs – so that eyes, for example, moved from side to side. Other slides were worked by means of a lever, which moved one of the discs up

and down. This would, for example, blot out the rope above a skipping man's head while making a new rope appear beneath his feet; if the lever was moved rapidly up and down, the man actually seemed to be skipping.

The most advanced of the special-effect slides was the rackwork slide, in which the Victorian fascination with gears came into full play. The basic mechanism was a toothed rack, along which a worm-screw moved to direct one of the discs – usually round a circle – when the crank was turned. The most sophisticated rackwork slides also had a tab on the other side, allowing it to be pulled or worked up and down to give a separate effect. In one very well known example, the tab works a man's jaws open and shut while the crank action sends a series of rats leaping into his mouth.

Still other idiosyncratic and charming optical effects were created by a form of rackwork slide called a Chromatrope, which was still on sale for use in magic lanterns at least sixty years after its first appearance in the mid-nineteenth century. As in other special slides, the Chromatrope contained two glass discs, one superimposed on the

other; but the difference was that they were linked by wires arranged on a pulley that was attached to a crank at the side of the frame. Each disc was painted with an abstract coloured pattern; when the crank was turned, the discs moved in opposite directions so that the lantern's light threw shifting 'Chromatropic' ('colour-turning') patterns on to the wall or screen. Similar light-effects – more all-embracing but generally less subtle – have been popular in discos over the past few years.

The black-and-white forerunner of the Chromotrope was the Eidotrope ('Turning image'), in which the discs were made of metal, with designs, in the form of small holes, punched on them. The turning of the discs in front of the lamp opened and closed little areas of light on the screen, making constantly shifting patterns – a cross between the effects of the Spirograph and of the Op Art so much admired in the 1960s.

In many respects, these two abstract slides, the Chromatrope and the Eidotrope, provided the most satisfactory representations of movement. Other attempts, though often admirable and ingenious, nevertheless relied on a willing suspension of disbelief on the part of the audience. In the long run, perhaps the slides with special effects were little more than novelties; perhaps the humble, static, single frames did a more solid job of entertaining and instructing. Accompanied by the right kind of narrative, generations of children enjoyed fables of all kinds – whether about 'The Three Bears' or 'Our Indian Empire' – without experiencing the least difficulty in making the mental journey from one frame to the next. And, of course, the magic lantern is still with us – transformed into slide projectors or, on a different scale, into pocket-sized viewers.

Toys producing kinetic effects, also popular in the Victorian period, derived from genuine

Opposite
An engraving of E. G. Robertson's
Phantasmagoria.

Right
Revolving transfer-printed glass
lantern slides. German. *c.* 1890.
Bethnal Green Museum, London.

Below
These mechanical penny-in-the-slot
printed-tin machines dispensed
chocolate. The machines are by (*left
to right*): Felix Potin; Stollwerck of
Cologne, (this machine is also a
savings bank, their bank 'for the
obedient child'); dispenser by K.B. of
Paris. Private collection.

French magic lantern made of tin with glass lenses. Manufactured in the first half of the 19th cent. Height: 33.02 cm (13.2 in). Bethnal Green Museum, London.

phenomenon which led to momentous consequences – ultimately, the whole history of the cinema, for the most sophisticated films are ultimately no more than a succession of phased, still photographs shown at high speed.

An ever-popular toy and a precursor to the animated film, which has embodied the principle for well over a century, is the pack of cards or booklet riffled with the thumb to show 'moving pictures'. However, the first conscious exploitation of persistence of vision was the Thaumatrope, devised and marketed under the slogan, *Vide et Crede* ('See It and Believe It'), by Dr. John Paris of Penzance less than two years after the theory was developed. The Thaumatrope consisted of a circular card with a different picture on each side. When the pieces of string which were attached to each edge were twisted between forefinger and thumb, the card spun round and the two pictures merged to form a single design. The illusion was not literally one of movement but of simultaneity – of bird and cage, known to be in separate places, appearing to occupy the same place at the same time. There was, so to speak, a purely mental movement, of the bird into the cage, of performers into the proscenium of a toy theatre, of a jockey on to a horse, a fish into a tank, and so on. Incidentally, the original British Thaumatrope cards threw in the most excruciating riddling jokes for extra value: side one: picture of bald man with the caption, 'Why does this man appear over head and ears in debt?'; Side two: picture of wig with caption, 'Because he has not paid for his wig'. The very introduction of the invention, written by Dr. Paris and printed inside the lid of the box, is an extended pun on the rotating quality of the toy:

'one good turn deserves another', and [the inventor] trusts that his discovery may afford the happy

advances in optical theory that were made in the early nineteenth century. The clue to achieving a convincing illusion of movement was provided by a scientific principle discovered in 1824. This was the persistence of vision, announced to the Royal Society in London by Dr. P. M. Roget, now better remembered as the instigator of Roget's *Thesaurus*. The persistence of vision simply means that an object brought into the field of vision will make an impression on the retina, and that that impression remains for a few moments after the object itself has been removed. From the point of view of kinetic devices, the breakthrough came when inventors realised that a second (different) object could be presented to the eye before the image of the first had faded: if the second object differed from the first only in some small detail, the succession of slightly changed (phased) images would give an illusion of movement. Persistence of vision, once identified, was a

120

means of giving activity to wit that has long been stationary, of revolutionizing the present system of standing jokes, and of putting into rapid circulation the most approved bon-mots.

The first device to give the illusion of continuous movement was invented in 1832 by two men working independently of each other. Joseph Antoine Ferdinand Plateau, a dedicated Belgian investigator of optics, invented the Phenakistoscope; while Simon von Stampfer, a Viennese professor, called his identical discovery the Stroboscope. These and other outlandish names of this sort (Cycloscope/Stereoscope, Graphoscope, Debusscope, Charimorphoscope, Chromeidoscope and Pheusitrope), which bedevil the subject, and seem to reflect an attitude of whimsical, mock self-importance, were made up from Greek or Latin elements: Thaumatrope ('spinning wonder'), Phenakistoscope ('deceptive viewer'), Stroboscope ('whirling viewer'). We still use some equally outlandish expressions, such as cinematography ('motion drawing') and cinemascope, but we have grown too accustomed to them to notice their peculiarity.

The earliest form of Phenakistoscope (or Stroboscope) consisted of a disc with phased drawings round the circumference: children on a see-saw, a couple dancing, a man jumping up and down on a tight-rope – all perpetual-motion sequences, going on round and round without beginning or end. A series of narrow slots were made on the disc, cut from or just below the circumference, and aligned with the little pictures. The viewer stood in front of a mirror holding the disc – with the picture side of the 'scope' away from him – by the wooden handle fixed perpendicularly to its centre. When he twirled the disc and looked through the slots at the mirror, the children see-sawed,

the couple danced, and the tight-rope walker jumped up and down – all thanks to the persistence of vision. The centres of most discs of this type sported fanciful abstract decorations which also melted into each other when the disc was spun round.

If the early Phenakistoscope is an elegant little object, the later 'improved' version is less

Top
Church Army magic lantern. English. *c.* 1920. Bethnal Green Museum, London.

Above
Handpainted (oil on glass) magic lantern slide in a wooden frame. English. Late 19th cent. When the lantern is operated, the wheel at the centre is shown turning. Bethnal Green Museum, London.

attractive. It dispenses with the need for a mirror by transferring the slots to a second disc placed over the one with pictures; the two are simply spun together to give the effect of movement. Its inventor, an Austrian army officer named von Uchatius, also experimented with a combination of the Phenakistoscope and magic lantern which furthered the development of the cinema.

A more elaborate version of the Plateau-Stampfer invention was produced within a year or so by an English showman named Horner, but his Daedelum (named after the mythical Greek inventor Daedalus) made no commercial impact until it was re-introduced in the 1860s as the Zoetrope or (in neat translation) Wheel of Life. This cylindrically-shaped object consisted of a stationary outer wall, pierced by a series of slits, inside which was a movable drum upon which the picture strip was arranged. The drum turned on a pin held up by a sturdy base that might consist of several heavy-furniture-style feet – the impression is of an odd-looking table lamp with a peculiar slotted cardboard or metal shade. The viewer simply spun the drum and then looked through a slit while the picture strip revolved. This system possessed several advantages over its precursors. Not only could an

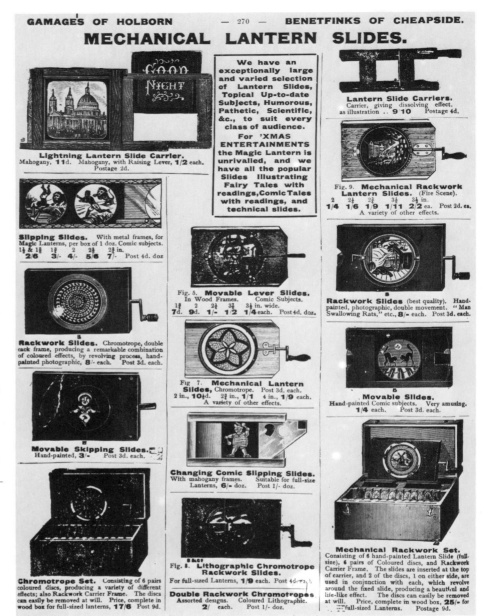

Above
1913 Gamage's catalogue illustrating various types of magic lantern slides.

Left
Chromotrope made by Carpenter and Westley. English. Science Museum, London.

Opposite
Phenakistoscope (or phantascope) encased in a mahogany box; and phenakistoscope discs. English. c. 1834. Bethnal Green Museum, London.

Below
Five phenakistoscope discs. Science
Museum, London.

Bottom
Phenakistoscope box lid. Science
Museum, London.

infinite number of 'shows' be put
on since the picture strips were
cheap and could be easily and
quickly changed, but also, several
people could watch the same
show simultaneously, each
stationed in front of a different
slot. Furthermore, the Zoetrope
was no mere frivolous paper toy
but a widely enjoyed and durable
source of entertainment. At least

one surviving example was made
to be driven by a little steam
engine, which must have been
quite expensive to produce, but,
at the other extreme, miniature
penny versions were also
produced.

In the United States, the
Zoetrope was patented in 1867 by
Milton Bradley. Some years later
he sold a haberdashery company
the right to market a Zoetrope
Collar Box: when the collars were
taken out, the round box itself
became the Zoetrope. Three
picture strips were given away as
part of the package, which
retailed at a total cost of twenty
cents.

The next optical development
was the work of a gifted
Frenchman, Emile Reynaud, a
professor of natural science who
had a flair for showmanship. At
the 'Optical Theatre' productions
he put on at the Musée Grevin in
Paris in the 1890s, Reynaud
showed colour 'movies' with
synchronised sound effects that
belong to what C. W. Ceram calls
the 'archaeology of the cinema'.
The basic device he used, the
Praxinoscope ('action viewer'),
which Reynaud patented as early
as 1877, was also a toy for the
home. This invention retained the
Zoetrope's drum-and-picture-
strip arrangement, but dispensed
with the viewing slits. Instead, the
viewers looked at the drum hub,
which was faceted with mirrors,
each mirror reflecting one of the
phased pictures on the strip. The
resulting image was far clearer
and less distorted than the
Zoetrope's, and had the further
advantage of being able to be seen
at evening performances, thanks
to the candle holder attached to
the top of the hub. The most
sophisticated form of the
Praxinoscope, the Praxinoscope
Theatre, was encased in a sturdy
box that opened up to make a
viewing apparatus. When the
viewer looked through a
horizontal rectangular slot in the
top of the box, he saw part of a
wooden board painted to look like
a theatre proscenium with

columns, curtains, and a framed stage at the centre of which was another slot through which a picture-strip figure could be seen. When the drum was set in motion the figure gave a convincing 'stage' performance.

In 1897, Herman Casler, an American, adapted the simple flicker-book principle to a machine called the Mutoscope ('changing-viewer') which used phased photographs instead of pictures. The machines, housed in massive, ornate iron cases, and operated by depositing a coin and then cranking a handle to flick the photographs, soon became a craze. In the United States, there were Mutoscope parlours in most of the larger towns. In Britain, the machines were above all seaside entertainments. Many of them remained in operation for decades, surviving on piers and in arcades for a good many years after the Second World War. As late as the 1960s, C. W. Ceram sighted Mutoscopes still in operation on Hamburg's well-known Reeperbahn, which is not exactly a children's playground: one of the shows was called 'When Women Become Hyenas'; its companion-piece was called 'The Mouse at a Tea Party'. Ceram also found Mutoscopes in the United States, on Broadway, and on Coney Island during roughly the same period.

In 1898, a toy with the same flicker-book basis was patented as the Filoscope. This was like an inexpensive version of a Mutoscope, consisting as it did of a handy-sized, pleasantly decorative metal case and a lever-release device that allowed the photographs to flicker past. A small portable version of the Mutoscope was also sold as a toy for the wealthy: the Kinora (*kine*, 'motion', rounded off with a meaningless flourish). In 1903, it was advertised in the *Illustrated London News* as:

'*The Latest and Greatest Achievement in Animated Photography . . . so lifelike as to*

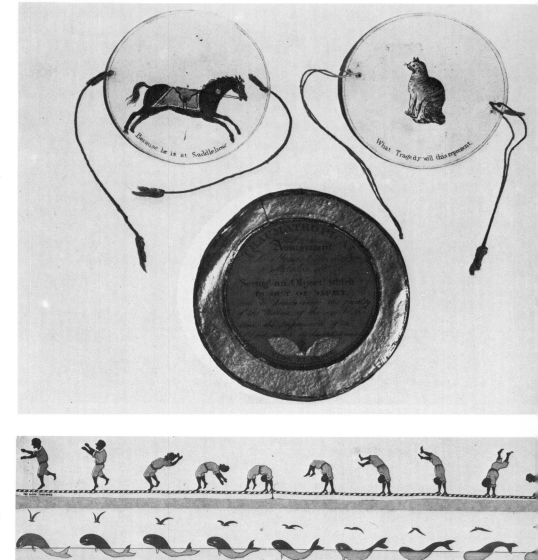

Top
Thaumatrope discs. Science Museum, London.

Above
Zoetrope strips showing the development of movement. English. *c.* 1850. Museum of London.

Left
Zoetrope. English. Late 19th cent. Museum of London.

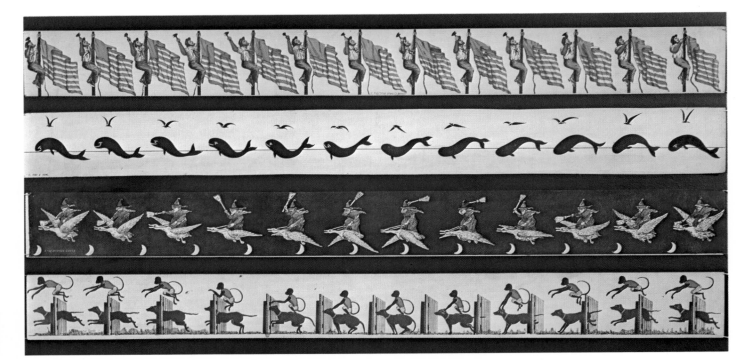

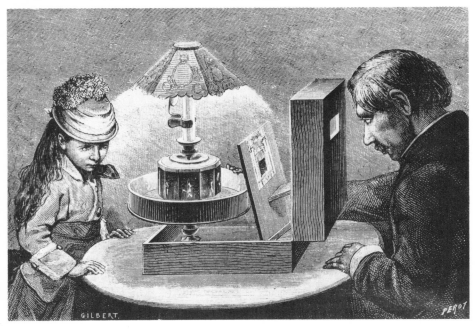

Above
Engraving of Reynaud's
Praxinoscope theatre.

Right
A Marey zoetrope. E. J. Marey, a
French physiologist, was responsible
for developing and improving various
types of fast-action cameras which
enabled him to get photographs of
the development of body movements.
His photographic gun recorded
pictures on a revolving disk
somewhat like a zoetrope disc.
Science Museum, London.

*border on the marvellous'. £3 3s
[£3.15] [complete with
picture reel]* ; '*Picture Reels
exchanged on the Library System*'.

An associated advertisement
hawked Animated Family
Portraits which could be obtained
from The Biograph Studio in
Regent Street:

*This is the only method by which the
actual gesture, expression, smile,
and other characteristics can be
reproduced. The studio is equipped
with an installation of electric light
which is unparalleled in the history
of photography, and by the aid of
which photographs may be taken in
any light by day or night. A reel of
upwards of 600 photographs costs
£2 2s [£2.10] ; repeat order 15s
[£0.75].*

Technically speaking, devices
such as the Praxinoscope and the
Kinora were step-children to the
cinema, a subject whose further
development lies outside the scope
of this book. But film projectors
for children – fully operational toys
– were on sale as early as 1899.
Only in the twentieth century,
however, have such sophisticated
toys been technically adequate,
whatever their novelty appeal.

Modern Developments

Many of the main twentieth-century trends were already visible before the turn of the century. Clockwork and friction-driven toys had become amazingly sophisticated; electricity was being more and more widely used; and the popularity of most model and construction sets was well established, although there was one great British firm that was just starting to make headway by the beginning of the First World War. This sprang from the idea of Frank Hornby, a Liverpool office worker who entertained his children by making metal parts from which they could construct machines. In 1901 he patented the idea under the title Mechanics Made Easy, and it was known as such until 1907, when its present familiar name, Meccano, was adopted. Wittingly or otherwise, Hornby had chosen his moment well: Meccano appeared when educational theorists were beginning to advocate learning by doing, and when the British were regularly being told that their scientific education was lamentably inferior to the German system. Meccano itself had the additional advantage that children liked it.

In the next few decades Hornby, along with the other firms, took advantage of some major advances: the further development of mass-production

methods, the still wider application of electricity (especially batteries), and the development of new synthetic materials – plastic and other synthetics – that were to revolutionize the whole toy industry. In 1915, the Hornby name itself became public property when its now-famous clockwork and electric train sets came on to the market. Like

Hornby 'Flying Scotsman' 4472 electric-powered train made of pressed steel. *c.* 1930. The station platform is by Meccano of Liverpool. *c.* 1925. Bethnal Green Museum, London.

Meccano display model of a
showman's traction engine. The
firebox conceals an electric motor
with chain-drive attached to the front
and rear wheels. Made of red, blue,
and gilt-coloured Meccano pieces.
Length: 75 cm (30 in). Sotheby's,
London.

Bassett-Lowke's trains, these were
more accurate than their German
equivalents, but the Hornby
versions were cheaper tinplate
models aimed at a far wider
market than Bassett-Lowke had
reached. The efficiency with
which Hornby reproduced every
model in sight gave the firm
another advantage: its
comprehensive range challenged
enthusiasts to keep on buying in
order to have complete sets
relevant to a particular type or
period. Later still, just before his
death in 1934, Frank Hornby
started another well-known line,
Dinky Toys, which is still going
strong. In recent years the
traditional Meccano set has been
joined by Plastic Meccano and by
Prima, a pre-school construction
toy. Hornby Hobbies (now part of
the Rovex Group) are still putting
out new and improved
locomotives as well as Scalectrix,
the remote-control car racing
system.

Soon after the First World
War, there was a change in the

international order that proved
permanent. In the 1920s the
United States became the leading
toymaking nation, at least in
terms of quantity, and she has
never since lost that position –
although Japan is a close rival.
The German industry recovered
from the war with remarkable
speed, and for a time even
challenged the Americans again
in their own market, but it was
American tariffs on imported
toys, not the war, that broke the
German's grip. Behind the tariff
shield, which gave them the run
of their huge home market,
American manufacturers
developed mass-production and
distribution techniques that also
enabled them to invade overseas
markets.

It was in this period that Louis
Marx & Co. of New York thrust
ahead to become the largest
toymaking firm in the world, with
subsidiaries in many other
countries. Marx was above all a
commercial enterprise, selling
directly to Woolworth's and other

big stores, and concentrating on the business of making almost every kind of toy cheaper and in larger quantities than its competitors, many of which fell by the wayside and were taken over by their successful rival. Marx made huge numbers of clockwork and friction-driven tin toys and it also moved into the clockwork and electrical train business, producing models that were less accurate and detailed than those of Lionel, Hornby and similar firms, but quite substantially cheaper. This proved to be another commercially inspired stroke, opening up a market whose existence had previously been unsuspected. Later, like other firms, Marx turned mainly to plastic toys, but mechanical tin toys continued to be made in the United States and Western Europe with a high degree of skill and inventiveness, and in this sphere the Germans retained their old mastery.

Between the wars, Japan also entered the market, although her products at this time showed little individuality. Then, during the Second World War, as in the First, toy manufacturers found their markets gone and their plants turned over to war production. For Germany, the position was doubly serious after 1945 as a result of the East–West split: Brandenburg and Thuringia became part of East Germany (eventually the G.D.R.), while the Bavarian centres were in the Western zones (eventually the Federal Republic). For Nuremberg and Fürth, being in the American zone was a stroke of good fortune, since American money got the toy factories going again and the United States provided a ready market for the goods. The Japanese industry was also rebuilt with American help, and both Germans and Japanese produced splendidly colourful tin toys from the 1950s to the 1970s. If the Japanese reputation had been for rather shoddy copies before the War, in the 1960s and '70s it was they who generally produced more sophisticated and finished metal toys – clockwork or battery-powered – than other countries. At the time of writing, the outlook for tin toys seems bleak owing to rising labour costs and successful competition from plastic, although the U.S.S.R. and East European countries evidently find it economic to keep on producing and exporting. Epitaphs for this colourful aspect of toymaking might yet prove premature. Indeed, some tin toys, like other toy-antiques which have been lovingly collected, are now being

Below
Rear: Hornby Gauge 'O', 1185 LMS Compound, the No. 2 special train with Pullmans Loraine and Arcadia. 1930s. *Front:* Hornby 0-4-0 LMS No. 1 tank engine pulling various private company goods vans. *c.* 1920s. The milk churns and Hall's Distemper sign are also by Hornby. Private collection.

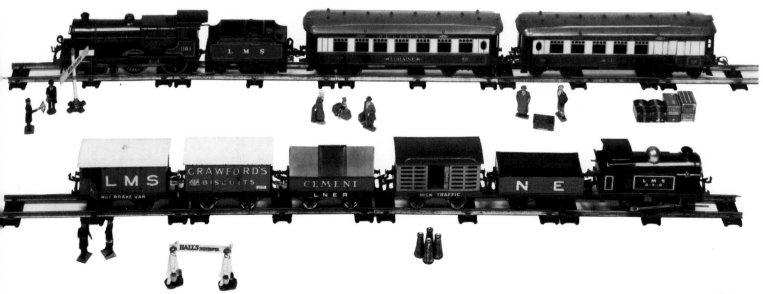

Above
This group of Minic toys, made by Lines Brothers of London between 1930-40, are similar to Hornby's early Dinky Toys. Museum of London.

Left
Three models of landspeed record breaking cars, made by the Kingbury Manufacturing Co. of America. *Left to right:* The Sunbeam (1927), the Bluebird (1928) and the Golden Arrow (1929). Bethnal Green Museum, London.

Above
Three American toys from the 1930s.
Gertie the Galloping Goose, by
Unique Art Manufacturing Co. of
Newark, New Jersey; Height:
23.5 cm (9.4 in). The Running
Scottie and the Running Spaniel,
both by Marx, New York. Bethnal
Green Museum, London.

Right
Clockwork tin turkey which struts and
displays its tail. German. 1948-
52. Bethnal Green Museum,
London.

Like

Like

Opposite Top
Three novelty action toys of the 1930s. Sparks fly from the train's funnel when movement is activated. Private collection.

Opposite Bottom
An aluminium and tin van made by Chad Valley in the 1940s, advertising their board games; and a streamlined racing car made by Wells in the 1930s. Both English. Private collection.

Above
Trains by Marx of New York, both of which were samples from the firm's archives. 1930s. The Union Pacific streamline train is 26 cm (10.4 in) long. Bethnal Green Museum, London.

reproduced. Steam-driven toy trains, for example, are more than antiquarian fads: thanks to western affluence (and despite all economic crises) they have reappeared in the toyshops. Another old favourite, the iron mechanical bank, has been reproduced but remains too expensive for children to afford, even in the garishly painted version from Taiwan.

Clockwork and friction-driven toys also show no signs of disappearing; in fact they are being adapted to many of the strong wooden toys made for pre-school children but electricity has gradually taken over as the chief motive power of mechanical toys. Early in the century, the leaky wet-cell battery was replaced by the safer, more efficient dry-cell battery, which made electric toys a much more attractive proposition; and when plastic came along in the 1950s, batteries became the natural power source for mechanical toys of all sizes. Then, with the spread of electricity to homes and the development of the transformer, electric toy train systems run directly from the mains were made possible. There was also a significant change in train models: gauges became not only

progressively more accurate but also smaller – a development that made sense in a world where people often lacked space. The table-top modeller is now at least as well catered for as the addict with a whole room to spare for his hobby.

The popularity of general construction sets was greater than ever after the First World War. Construction kits for building clockwork cars began to be made, notably by Meccano and Märklin. The first clockwork cars and aeroplanes built exactly to scale were made in the early 1930s – the cars were even submitted to a miniature hill test in the factories! Meccano had a firm grip on the European market and also established an agency in the United States, but there the firm ran into powerful competition from Erector, a construction kit marketed by the A. C. Gilbert Company of New Haven, Connecticut. In comparison with Meccano's flat metal rods with lines of holes for bolts, Erector components, with their girder-like appearance, had the advantage of making some constructions (for example, bridges) look more realistic. Erector also gained advantage over Meccano by featuring a motor with which to

Above
Four soldiers in a jeep, Marx of New York. 1940s. Length: 14 cm (5.6 in). Private collection.

Left
Police motorcycle with sidecar and working siren. Clockwork mechanism. Marx of New York. 1940s. Length: 21 cm (8.4 in). Private collection.

Opposite Top
Rear: liner by Fleischman. 1930-1950. It came in a variety of sizes. Length: 33 cm (13.2 in). *Front:* liner by Carette. *c.* 1900. Imitation smoke winds the clockwork. The rower is by Bing. *c.* 1920. Private collection.

Opposite Bottom
Charlie Chaplin, who is made to swing his cane, was made in Germany. *c.* 1930. The other toys, which all raise and lower their arms while their bodies vibrate, were made by Shuco of Nuremberg. *c.* 1935. Bethnal Green Museum, London.

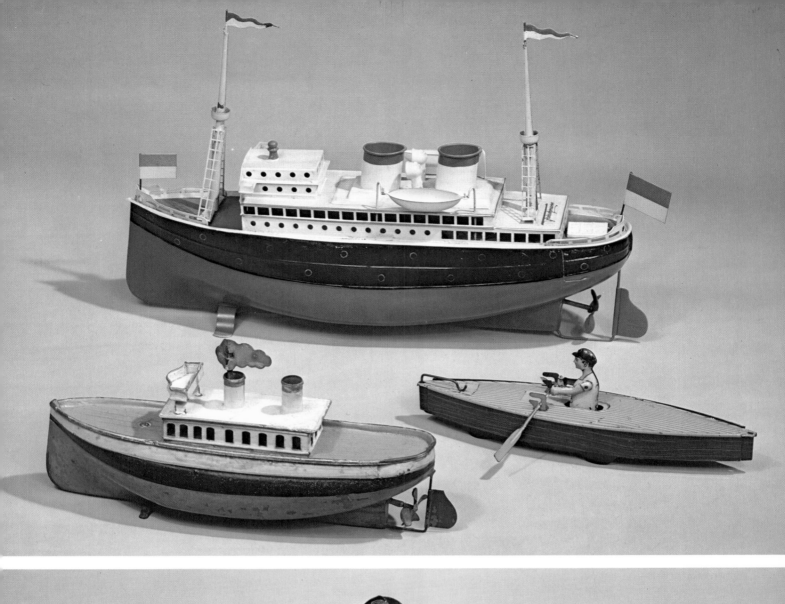

Shuco
Nuremberg
1935

run models. Fighting on home territory, Gilbert conducted a vigorous and successful promotion campaign, for a time making nationwide tours in a special Gilbert Toys railroad car. The result was that Meccano ultimately sold out their American interest to Gilbert.

Among the greatest successes of the post-war period is Lego, the interlocking plastic brick construction toy which was devised and marketed in 1951 by Gotfred Kirk Christiansen, the son of a toymaker. Since then, Lego has enjoyed such world-wide popularity that almost 99 per cent of its sales are made outside its country of origin, Denmark. (*Leg* is Danish for 'play'.) The early design-it-yourself packs have been increasingly supplemented by pre-designed kits with motors, gears, lights, pistons and other mechanical features, in this

Above
Back Left: Tank by Marx of New York. 1938. 205.74 × 11.17 × 13.97 cm (9 × 4 × 5 in). *Back Right:* a cast-lead searchlight. The 4 volt bulb can be operated by batteries. English. *c.* 1915. *Front Left to Right:* Anti-aircraft gun, naval gun, howitzer. All by William Britain & Sons. English. *c.* 1940. Bethnal Green Museum, London.

Opposite Top
Gunboat, 22.8 cm (9 in) long, and attendant flotilla of three submarines. German. Christie's, London.

Opposite Bottom
Toys by Shuco of Nuremberg. German. 1935-37. Height 13 cm (5.2 in). Sotheby's, London

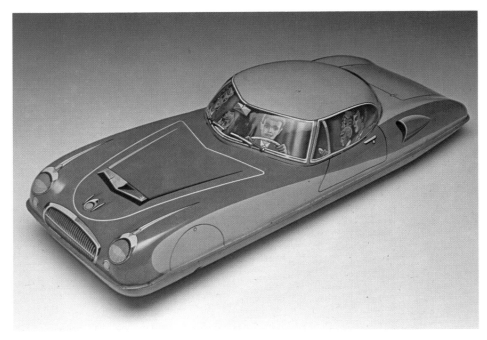

Above
The 'Nippy Shillings Worth' was
made in Germany. c. 1930. (Lyon's
fast-food waitresses were known as
'Nippies'). Lehmann's Autobus was
an exceptionally popular toy which
sold in large quantities before and
after World War II. Private collection.

Left
A family saloon car made in West
German. 1950s. Length : 33 cm
(13.2 in). Private collection.

Opposite Top
Three friction-driven cars made by
Haji of Japan. 1950s. Length : 10 cm
(4 in). Private collection..

Opposite Bottom
Friction-driven motorscooter made by
Technofix of West Germany. c. 1950.
Length : 16.5 cm (6.6 in). Private
collection.

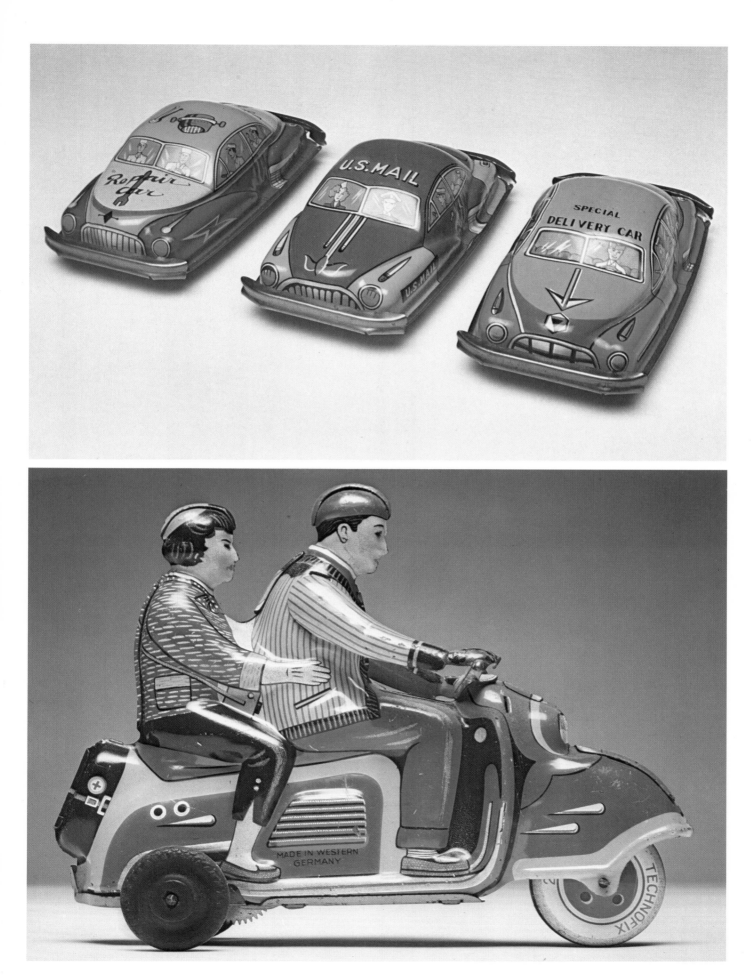

Left
Friction-driven aeroplane by Shuco of Nuremberg. German. *c.* 1935. Length: 9 cm (3.6 in). Sotheby's, London.

Below
Distler aeroplanes. The monoplane loops the loop as it is rotated by the pylon. The late 1930s passenger plane is friction-driven. Private collection.

A tinplate motorcycle, made by K. Arnold & Co. of Nuremberg. *c.* 1950. The rider mounts and drives off, and then dismounts by means of a clockwork mechanism. A start/stop control is on one side. Length : 20 cm (8 in). Sotheby's, London.

respect following the pattern of Erector and other construction toys. The sheer inclusiveness of the Lego range is impressive, as is the professionalism with which the spares service offers replacements for everything from power units to weighted keels. Lego continues to be made in Billund, a small village in the middle of Jutland. Instead of leaving the village for somewhere more cosmopolitan, Christiansen brought the world to Billund : in 1968 he created Legoland, a splendid amusement park that is also a non-stop advertisement for the product. Almost every object in the park is made of Lego bricks or looks as though it is, with its surface 'studded' in characteristic Lego style. There are Lego villages, palaces, and castles; harbours and boats; a railway

station, an airport, a miniature version of Cape Kennedy; a Red Indian reservation, a Wild-Western town, and a 'town of the future' which is impressively clean and has an alien look when lit up at night. Children can tour the park in an electric train or go up in the air by Legocopter (operated by a hydraulic lift). There is even a traffic school in which eight- to fourteen-year-olds can drive electric cars with brakes and signals; then, after a course of instruction, they take (and invariably pass) their driving tests; and at the end they receive Legoland driving licences.

As an idea, Legoland owes a great deal to Disneyland, the even more grandiosely conceived park set up by Walt Disney in Anaheim, California, in 1955. Here too there are guided train tours,

Left
Battery-driven superjet made by TN
of Japan in the 1960s. The pilot
swivels his gun when the toy is in
motion. Length: 31 cm (12.4 in).
Private collection, London.

Below
Group of friction-driven aeroplanes
made by various Japanese
manufacturers in the 1960s and
1970s. Average length: 10 cm (4 in).
Private collection, London.

Opposite Top
Meccano motor car construction kit.
The tyres, pressed mild steel body
frame, wheels, running boards,
radiator and seats were all provided
with the instruction book. *c.* 1935.
Bethnal Green Museum, London.

Opposite Bottom
Friction-driven flying saucer made by
Man Ubishi of Japan in the 1960s.
Width: 17 cm (6.8 in). Private
collection, London.

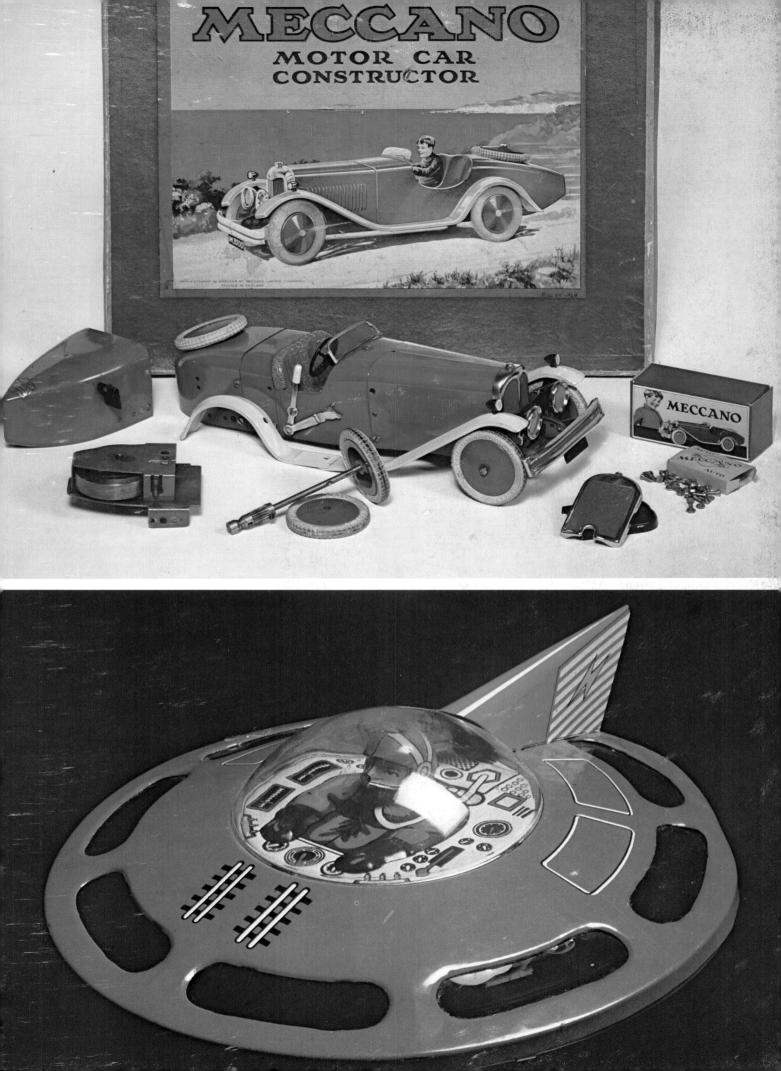

Right
Musical clockwork-operated Pluto
and Donald Duck Disney toys made
by Marx of New York. 1930s.
Sotheby's, London.

Below
Cast-metal battery-operated 'Electro
Take-apart' fire engine by Shuco of
Nuremberg. Length: 35.5 cm (14 in).
Christie's, London.

running through a diorama of the
Grand Canyon as well as various
other settings inspired by Walt
Disney cartoons and films; rides
and sails, including a trip on an
'atomic' submarine; and all sorts
of supplementary entertainments
mechanical and otherwise. Walt
Disney Productions' other park,
Disney World, whose theme is
The Magic Kingdom, is located
in Orlando, Florida. A separate
attraction, the Experimental
Prototype Community of
Tomorrow, is planned for 1982.
The first phase of this project will
consist of a Future World, which
will include various pavilions
devoted to all aspects – past,
present and future – of life on
earth and in space; and a World
Showcase, a kind of international
world fair. Undoubtedly, a vast
amount of new mechanical toys
will emerge from a project of this
magnitude, especially toys
reflecting future means of
transportation and aspects of
everyday life on earth and in
space.

Among the new mechanical
dolls of the century are the
beating-heart doll and the
praying doll created in the 1940s.
Within a few years the first plastic
dolls appeared, but they were
soon followed by dolls made of
other synthetic materials which
combined relative cheapness and
improved hygiene with
capabilities of greater accuracy.
Vinyl in particular was a suitably
flexible material and lent itself to
realistic tinting. In the 1960s,
western affluence made it possible
to find buyers for quite elaborate
speaking and singing dolls, now
given vocal powers by tape
recorders or transistors. Electric
batteries powered a variety of
movements – crawling, walking,
pushing and pulling – but perhaps
the most impressive of all the
moving dolls was Mattel's
Dancerina, which performed on
points and pirouetted to the
strains of Tchaikovsky's 'Dance of
the Sugar Plum Fairy'. Among
other new developments are
weeping dolls, kissing dolls, dolls

that can acquire a tan, and even (for the social realist sensibility) dolls that belch.

Since 1958 there have been some entirely new subjects as well: the adult doll with working accessories such as battery-driven bedside lamps, hair dryers, and even shampoo parlours which take advantage of the fact that modern dolls come with hair fixed firmly into their plastic scalps. Casdon, for example, make a line of fair-sized plastic-and-metal kitchenware including a sink-unit and battery-operated cookers and washing machines. A doll made for boys was also produced and promoted in similar style, with an ever-growing collection of accessories. The pioneers in this field were Hassenfeld Brothers, who in 1964 brought out G.I. Joe, later known as Action Man when his roles became multi-national. Action Man, with his

Above
Mickey Mouse tinplate clockwork organ-grinder with Mickey operating the organ and Minnie dancing on top. Probably made by Distler. German. *c.* 1930. Sotheby's, London.

Right
Merry Makers' mouse orchestra by Marx of New York. American. Width: 22.5 cm (9 in). This tinplate clockwork toy was probably inspired by Disney. Christie's, London.

Overleaf
A family of clockwork robots, all made in Japan in the 1960s-70s. The tallest is 19 cm (7.6 in). Private collection.

realistic hair, scarred cheek, gripping hands, and moving 'Eagle' eyes, can be kitted out as a serviceman in any of the main Second World War armies, or as a skin diver, a mountaineer, or a Foreign Legionnaire. His equipment – helicopters, jeeps, bazookas and so on – works with varying degrees of realism and varies also in its accuracy in scale; perhaps the most impressive item is his machine-gun, which gives off ruby flashes as it rat-tat-tats. Eventually a talking Action Man was produced as were bearded Caucasian and bearded and non-bearded Negroid versions, along with Action Man books and records. There seems to be no end to the expansion of this particular line: the most recent addition is The Intruder, a palaeolithic hulk which is supposed to be the Action Man team's sworn enemy; when pressed between the shoulders he closes his arms in a bone-crunching grip. Other companies have produced variations on the Action Man idea, in various sizes and at various price levels, but the one word never used, of course, is 'doll': if the rumour ever reached boys that their 'movable fighting man' was really just a male doll, the trade might disappear overnight.

Many of the modern dolls are rather vapid-looking, the girls keeping a curiously sugar-'n-spice look that has been a feature of dolls since the Victorian period: the *kitsch* of the past, no longer omnipresent, become a subject for nostalgia. But, as if by some law of compensation, dolls and stuffed toys have also been the vehicles for a kind of gruesomeness that adults find equally difficult to accept. Again this is nothing new: Cruchet's *guillotine* entertained somebody around 1810, and reappeared alongside Sweeny Todd the throat-cutting barber in penny-in-the-slot pier shows; and grotesque dolls had a vogue early in the present century. Since the Second World War we have had Trolls, do-it-yourself Frankenstein's monsters, and –

the non-pareil – an Adolf Hitler who exclaims 'You can't win 'em all!', not to mention the frightening looking, multicoloured plastic robots which walk in characteristic lumbering fashion and fire off everything from missiles to parts of their own bodies.

The modern preoccupation with pre-school learning has also stimulated the production of small children's versions of adult appliances. Mattel, for example, put out a line of 'Tuff-Stuff' toys, advertised as being 'sturdy "play grown-up" toys, that look like the real thing!' Examples are the Play Vacuum and the Play Calculator, both working without batteries. The Wordwriter is a toy typewriter in which each of the seven keys types a separate word, but the words are chosen so that various permutations are possible, for example: I/We/You, See/Love Dad/Mom.

On the whole the tendency is towards greater realism in all things, from the little assassin's gun with silencer and telescopic sights to the astronaut's pedal moon-buggy; simplified or conventionalised toy-copies are mainly produced for very young children on the theory that this leaves more room for the exercise of imagination. Many educationalists are critical of the trend towards ever-greater realism because they fear it may kill imagination. They may of course be right, though in fact all toys leave something to the imagination and nobody has yet quantified the 'percentage' of imagination that gives a toy optimal value. In any event, realism is what the buyer – child or parent – seems to want just at the moment.

But there is one area in which fantasy still reigns over realism: the future. Wonderful whirring, light-flashing, space vehicles represent a view of future technology, albeit based on present achievements, and other space travel and science-future items are usually copies of science-fiction film and television concepts.

One exception is the solar toy devised by the American architect Charles Eames in the 1960s. This gave an appropriately futuristic display of whirling wheels and turning cranks, and was powered by electric energy stored up from sunshine by selenium cells in an aluminium reflector. Since the fuel crises of 1973–4 the whole idea has of course seemed far less implausible. If contemporary experiments with solar, tidal and wind energy ever pay off, there is every reason to suppose they will be applied to toys as well as other things. Here too fantasy may prove to be the first phase of creation.

Appendix A

MUSEUM COLLECTIONS

There are a surprisingly large number of museum collections with at least some mechanical toys. The general museums tend to be well situated; the specialized ones often less so, but well worth the journey. The list that follows is highly selective – no more than a starting point for the native or visiting enthusiast in some of the major toy-making countries.

England
Bethnal Green Museum, London
Pollock's Toy Museum, London
The Toy Museum, Rottingdean, Sussex

Scotland
Museum of Childhood, Edinburgh

Wales
Museum of Childhood, Menai Bridge

France
Conservatoire des Arts et des Métiers, Paris
Musée des Arts Décoratifs, Paris

German Federal Republic
Germanisches Nationalmuseum, Nuremberg

German Democratic Republic
Deutches Spielzeugmuseum, Sonneberg

Denmark
Hans Christian Andersen Family House and Museum, Odense

Switzerland
Musée d'Art et d'Histoire, Neuchâtel

Soviet Union
State Museum, Zagorsk

United States
Museum of the City of New York
New York Historical Society Museum

Canada
Band Collection, Metropolitan Toronto and Region Conservation
    Authority, Toronto

Appendix B

MAKERS OF MECHANICAL TOYS
The list that follows represents a small selection of known makers who started working before 1914. Those named are either famous in their own right or historically important as innovators in technique or mass-production methods. A few inventors, showmen, and similar figures are included for ease of reference.

Dates in brackets record the lifespan of an individual. Other dates refer to the *working* life of a person, family or firm.

Marks are not given: some makers used none, others (for example doll makers) used many. Business relations were often complicated, for example, by an independent designer working for a big firm on a particular project; by one firm representing another for a particular line; and by amalgamations, changes of name, etc. A reader who hopes to identify a doubtful item, or to follow the fortunes of a specific maker, should consult the specialist works cited in the Bibliography.

ALTHOF, BERGMANN & CO. Founded c. 1867. New York City, U.S.A. Manufactured clockwork and other toys.

AMERICAN TOY CO. 1869–72. New York City, U.S.A. Short-lived amalgamation of the George W. Brown of Connecticut and J. & E. Stevens companies.

ARNOLD, K., & CO. Founded 1906. Nuremberg, Germany. Manufactured mechanical toys; more recently specialised in model railways.

ARNOLD, OSCAR M. Neustadt, Germany. Doll maker.

BAKER, GEO., & CO. Geneva, Switzerland. Later Baker-Troll. Made musical boxes.

BASSETT-LOWKE & CO. Founded 1890. Northampton, Great Britain. Manufactured mechanical trains, often collaborating with Bing, Carette (qqv) and others.

BEGGS, EUGENE. 1870s. Paterson, New Jersey, U.S.A. Made toy steam engines.

BERTRAN, CHARLES. Paris, France. Doll maker: notable for swimming doll 1878.

BING, GEBRÜDER (BING BROTHERS). 1879–1933. Nuremberg, Germany. Maker of clockwork, steam and hot air toys; dolls; optical and kinetic toys.

BOLZ, LORENZ. Founded 1875. Zirndorf, Germany. Manufactured tin toys, notably tops.

BONTEMS. Family concern founded 1849. Paris, France. Luxurious musical toys and novelties; mechanical singing birds.

BRUGUIER FAMILY. Eighteenth–nineteenth century. Geneva, Switzerland. Made mechanical singing birds.

BRACHHAUSEN, GUSTAVE ADOLPH. Founder of the Regina Musical Box Company (qv).

BRADLEY, MILTON, CO. Founded 1860. Springfield, Massachusetts, U.S.A. Outstanding educational toy manufacturer. American patentee of Zoetrope.

BRITAIN, WILLIAM & SONS LTD. Founded 1840s. Walthamstow (originally Hornsey), London, England. Manufacturer of mechanical and other toys, notably hollow-cast lead soldiers.

BROWN, GEORGE W., & CO. 1856–1880s. Forestville (now Bristol), Connecticut, U.S.A. Manufactured the first clockwork toys made in the U.S.A. In 1869 merged his line of tin toys with the iron toys of J. & E. Stevens & Co. (q.v.). See also American Toy Company.

BRU, LÉON CASIMIR. Paris, France. Doll maker. Business carried on after his death by family members and others.

BUB, KARL. Founded 1851. Nuremberg, Germany. Manufactured mechanical toys, notably trains and cars; took over Bing (qv) in 1933.

BUCKMAN MANUFACTURING CO. Founded 1869. New York City, U.S.A. Made toy guns and steam engines.

CARETTE, GEORGES, ET CIE. 1886–1917. Nuremberg, Germany. Founded by a Frenchman, Georges Carette; manufactured mechanical toys and model trains.

CATTELAIN, F. Founded 1850. Geneva, Switzerland. Made mechanical singing birds.

CHAD VALLEY. Founded 1897. Harborne, Warwickshire, Great Britain. Manufacturers of clockwork toys and construction kits; best known for games.

CLAY, ROBERT. New York, U.S.A. Toy manufacturer; notable for 'creeping doll' patent 1871.

COX, JAMES (d. 1788). English maker of automata and clocks, exhibited at 'Cox's Museum' 1772–5.

DAWKINS, THOMAS, & CO. 1880–1914. Geneva, Switzerland. Made music boxes.

DOLL & CO. 1898–1938. Nuremberg, Germany. Manufactured toys, notably steam engines. Taken over by Fleischmann (qv).

DRESSEL, CUNO AND OTTO. Sonneberg, Germany. Doll makers.

EDISON, THOMAS ALVA (1847–1931). U.S.A. Inventor. In this context, notable for phonograph doll, patent 1878.

FABERGÉ, CARL (1846–1920). Russian jeweller, made Easter eggs and other items for Tsar and family, working with incredible skill in precious and semi-precious stones and metals. e.g. Trans-Siberian Railway Egg with platinum and gold clockwork train.

FAIVRE, EDMOND. 1860–1918(?). Paris, France. Manufactured mechanical toys and cars.

FLEISCHMANN, GEBRÜDER. Founded 1887. Nuremberg, Germany. Manufactured magnetic, clockwork and musical-box toys.

FLEISCHMANN & BLOEDEL. Paris, France. (Also traded as Joseph Berlin. Fürth, Nuremberg, Germany.) Doll makers.

GIRARD, PAUL. Paris, France. Doll maker, for some years linked with Bru (qv).

GONG BELL MANUFACTURING CO. Founded 1866. East Hampton, Connecticut, U.S.A. Notable for bell toys.

GRIESBAUM, KARL. Triberg, Germany. Made mechanical singing birds.

GUNTHERMANN, S. 1877–1965. Nuremberg, Germany. Manufactured clockwork toys.

HANDWERCKE, HEINRICH. Waltershausen, Germany. Doll maker.

HESS, MATTHEUS. 1826–1934. Nuremberg, Germany. Manufactured clockwork trains and cars, notably the Hessmobil.

HEUBACH, GEBRÜDER (HEUBACH BROTHERS). Coburg, Germany. Doll makers.

HILL BRASS COMPANY, N. N. Founded c. 1889. East Hampton, Connecticut, U.S.A. Notable for bell toys.

HODGSON, ELLEN. Inverness, Scotland. Doll maker: clockwork swimming doll 1896.

HÖLBE, RICHARD HUGO. Sonneberg, Germany. Doll maker.

HORNBY, FRANK. Created Meccano Limited 1901–64. Liverpool, Great Britain. Manufactured Meccano, clockwork and electric train sets, Dinky Toys. Hornby taken over by Lines (now Rovex Limited, Margate); Meccano Ltd. carries on at Liverpool.

HORNER, WILLIAM GEORGE (1786–1837). English showman, inventor of the 'Daedelum' optical device (later called Zoetrope).

IVES, EDWARD (1839–1918). Toy manufacturer at Plymouth, Connecticut, U.S.A.; founded E. R. IVES & CO. at Bridgeport, Connecticut 1870–1929; succeeded by son HARRY C. IVES. Firm also known variously as Ives, Blakeslee & Co. and Ives, Blakeslee & Williams. Major manufacturers of clockwork, iron and other toys.

JACQUES, WILLIAM W. Middlesex, Massachusetts, U.S.A. Doll maker: phonograph dolls 1888 and 1889.

JAQUET-DROZ, HENRI-LOUIS (1752–90). Geneva, and Paris, France. Son of Pierre Jaquet-Droz (qv). Maker of automata of many kinds, musical clocks, etc.

JAQUET-DROZ, PIERRE (1721–90). La Chaux de Fonds, Switzerland. Maker of automata of many kinds, musical clocks, etc.

JEP. 1899–1965. Paris, France. Made mechanical toys. Originally called 'Société Industrielle de Ferblanterie' (SIF), later Jouets de Paris, finally Jep.

JOUETS DE PARIS, LES. See Jep.

JUMEAU, EMILE. Paris, France. Doll maker.

KÄMMER & REINHARDT. Waltershausen, Germany. Doll makers.

KEMPELEN, BARON WOLFGANG VON (1734–1804). Austrian inventor of automata; also of the pseudo-automaton chess player 'The Turk'.

LA FOSSE, MARIE LAMBERT. Paris, France. Doll maker.

LAMBERT, T. B. England. Doll maker.

LE ROY. Nineteenth century. Paris, France. Made musical boxes and clocks with automata.

LECOULTRE FRÈRES. Early nineteenth century. Geneva, Switzerland. Made musical boxes.

LEHMANN, ERNST PAUL (d. 1934). Founded Brandenburg firm 1881. Succeeded by Johann Richter. Manufactured mechanical and other toys.

LIONEL ELECTRIC TRAIN CO. Founded 1906. New York, U.S.A. Manufactured electric trains and some other toys.

LOCHMANN, PAUL. Leipzig, Germany. Marketed first disc musical box, the Symphonion, 1885.

MAELZEL, JOHANN NEPOMUK (1770–1838). Austrian inventor of metronome, and panharmonicon and other automata; showed 'The Turk' chess pseudo-automaton.

MAILLARDET, HENRI (1745–?). Fontaines, Switzerland, and London, England. Apprenticed to Pierre Jaquet-Droz (qv). Maker of automata.

MAILLARDET, JEAN DAVID (1748–1808). Fontaines, Switzerland. Brother of Henri Maillardet (qv). Made singing birds and other automata.

MANGOLD, GEORG ADAM. Founded 1882. Fürth, Germany. Manufactured mechanical toys, from 1920s under the (still well-known) Gama trade mark.

MÄRKLIN, THEODORE F. (1817–66). German toy maker, from 1859 at Göppingen, Germany. Succeeded by wife Karoline and sons Karl, Wilhelm and Eugen; from 1892 Gebrüder Märklin & Cie. Mechanical toys, notably trains and construction kits.

MARSEILLE, ARMAND. Kopplesdorf, Germany. Doll maker.

MARTIN, E. Paris, France. Doll maker: patent for swimming doll 1876.

MARTIN, FERNAND. 1878–1912. Paris, France. Manufactured clockwork tin toys. Taken over by Bonnet & Cie.

MECCANO. See Hornby.

MERMOD, FRÈRES. 1815–89. St Croix, Switzerland. Maker of musical boxes and toys.

NICOLE-FRÈRES. 1839–1903. Geneva, Switzerland. Partnership formed by the brothers François and Raymond Nicole, working separately 1815–39. Makers of musical boxes of the finest quality.

PARIS, DR. JOHN AYRTON (1785–1856). Penzance, England. Devised and marketed the Thaumatrope, optical toy, 1826.

PAYÀ, HERMANOS. Founded 1906. Ibi, Spain. Manufactures mechanical trains and other toys

PINCHBECK, CHRISTOPHER (d. 1732). London, England. Made musical clocks; may have invented cylinder-and-comb principle for musical boxes.

PLANK, ERNST. 1866–1930s. Nuremberg, Germany. Manufactured clockwork and steam toys, especially trains.

PLATEAU, JOSEPH ANTOINE FERDINAND (1801–83). Belgian co-inventor (with Stampfer, qv) of the Phenakistoscope optical device.

POLYPHON MUSIC WORKS. 1889–1914. Leipzig, Germany. Makers of musical boxes.

REGINA MUSICAL BOX COMPANY. 1889–1921. Rahway, New Jersey, U.S.A. Pioneered mass-produced and self-changing disc musical boxes.

REYNAUD, EMILE (1844–1918). French inventor of the Praxinoscope optical device; also a cinematic pioneer.

ROBERT-HOUDIN, EUGÈNE (1805–71). French illusionist and maker of automata.

ROCHAT FAMILY. Early nineteenth century. Brassus and Geneva, Switzerland. Made mechanical singing birds.

ROITEL, CHARLES. 1880–1920s. Paris, France. Manufactured mechanical tin toys and steam engines.

ROSSIGNOL, CHARLES. 1868–1962. Paris, France. Manufactured mechanical toys.

SCHOENHUT, ALBERT, CO. Founded 1872. Philadelphia, U.S.A. Manufactured toy pianos, Humpty Dumpty Circus, etc.

SCHREYER & CO. Founded 1912. Nuremberg, Germany. Manufactured Schuco mechanical toys, notably cars.

SECOR, JEROME B. 1880s. Bridgeport, Connecticut, U.S.A. Maker of toy guns, locomotives; also of automata. Sold out to Ives (qv).

SIMON & HALBIG. Gotha, Germany. Doll makers.

SIF. See Jep.

SOCIÉTÉ FRANÇAISE DE FABRICATION DE BÉBÉS ET JOUETS. Paris, France. Toy and doll makers.

STAMPFER, SIMON VON. Austrian co-inventor (with Plateau, qv) of the Phenakistoscope optical device, which he called the Stroboscope.

STEINER, JULES NICHOLAS. Paris, France. Doll maker and mechanical toy maker.

STEVENS, J. & E., & CO. Founded 1843. Cromwell, Connecticut, U.S.A. Manufactured iron toys, notably mechanical banks. See also American Toy Company.

SYMPHONION COMPANY. See Lochmann.

TOWER TOY COMPANY. Founded 1830s. South Hingham, Massachusetts, U.S.A. Originally the Tower Guild, organised by William S. Tower. Probably the first substantial toy manufacturing concern in the U.S.A.

UCHATIUS, FRANZ VON (1811–81). Austrian inventor. Improved Phenakistoscope optical device; cinematic pioneer.

UNION MANUFACTURING CO. 1870s. Brooklyn, New York, U.S.A. Made toy steam engines.

VAUCANSON, JACQUES DE (1709–82). Grenoble and Paris, France. Maker of automata.

WATROUS, J. L., & CO. 1880s. East Hampton, Connecticut, U.S.A. Made iron and bell toys. Merged with Hill Brass Co. N. N. (qv).

WEBBER, RAND & GIVEN. U.S.A. Doll makers.

WEEDEN MANUFACTURING CO. Founded 1880s. New Bedford, Massachusetts, U.S.A. Notable for steam-driven toys.

WILKINS TOY CO. Founded 1888, developing out of the Triumph Wringer Company. Keene, New Hampshire, U.S.A. After 1919 known as Kingsbury Co.

Bibliography

Allemagne, Henri René d'. *Histoire des Jouets.* Paris 1903

Allemagne, Henri René d'. *Les Jouets à la World's Fair en 1904.* Paris 1908

Barenholtz, Edith (Ed.). *George Brown Toy Sketchbook.* U.S.A. 1972

Bassermann-Jordan, Ernst von. *Die Geschichte der Räderuhr.* Frankfurt am Main 1905

Britten, J. F. *Old Clocks and Watches and their Makers.* First edition London 1889; regularly brought up to date

Calmettes, Pierre. *Les Joujoux.* Paris 1924

Campardon, Emile. *Les Spectacles de la Foire.* Paris 1877

Ceram, C. W. *The Archaeology of the Cinema.* Translated by Richard Winston. London 1965

Chapuis, Alfred, and Edmund Droz. *Automata. A Historical and Technological study.* Translated by Alec Reid. London 1958

Claretie, Léo. *Les Jouets.* Paris 1893

Clark, John E. T. *Musical Boxes.* London (3rd ed.) 1961

Cook, Olive. *Movement in Two Dimensions.* London 1963

Cooke, Conrad William. *Automata, Old and New.* London 1893

Cox, James. A descriptive *Catalogue* of the several superb and magnificent pieces of mechanism and jewellery, exhibited in Mr Cox's museum. London 1772

Craig, Edward Gordon. *Gordon Craig's Book of Penny Toys.* Hackbridge 1899

Cremer, William Henry. *The Toys of the Little Folks of All Ages and Countries.* London 1873

Crowley, T. E. *Discovering Mechanical Music.* Aylesbury (Buckinghamshire, Great Britain) 1977

Daiken, Leslie. *Children's Toys Throughout the Ages.* London 1963

Ellis, R. *Great Exhibition of the Works of Industry of All Nations. Official Descriptive and Illustrated Catalogue.* 3 Vols. London 1851

Fraser, Antonia. *A History of Toys.* London 1966

Freeman, Ruth and Larry. *Cavalcade of Toys.* New York 1942

Gallon, M. *Machines et Inventions Approuvées par L'Académie des Sciences.* Paris 1735

Gordon, Leslie. *Peepshow into Paradise : A History of Children's Toys.* London 1953

Groeber, Karl. *Children's Toys of Bygone Days.* Translated by Philip Hereford. London 1932

Hertz, Louis H. *Messrs Ives of Bridgeport.* Wethersfield, Connecticut 1950

Hertz, Louis H. *The Toy Collector.* New York 1969

Hillier, Mary. *Pageant of Toys.* London 1965

Hillier, Mary. *Automata and Mechanical Toys.* London 1976

Holme, Geoffrey. *Children's Toys of Yesterday.* Special winter supplement of 'The Studio' (periodical). London 1932

McClintock, Marshall and Inez. *Toys in America.* Washington D.C. 1961

Maingot, Elaine. *Les Automates.* Paris 1959

Milet, Jacques. *Les Bateaux Jouets.* Paris 1967

Mosoriak, Roy. *The Curious History of Music Boxes.* Chicago 1943

Murray, Patrick. *Toys.* London 1968

Robert-Houdin, Jean Eugène. *Confidences et Révélations.* Blois 1868

Remise, Jacques, and Jean Fondin. *The Golden Age of Toys.* Lausanne 1967

Simmen, René. *Der Mechanische Mensch.* Zurich 1967

Tippett, James S. *Toys and Toymakers.* New York 1931

Toy Manufacturing Association. *Toy Manufacturers in the U.S.A.* New York 1935

Weltens, Arno. *Mechanical Tin Toys in Colour.* Poole (Dorset, Great Britain) 1977

White, Gwen. *European and American Dolls.* London 1966

White, Gwen. *Toys, Dolls, Automata : Marks and Labels.* London 1975

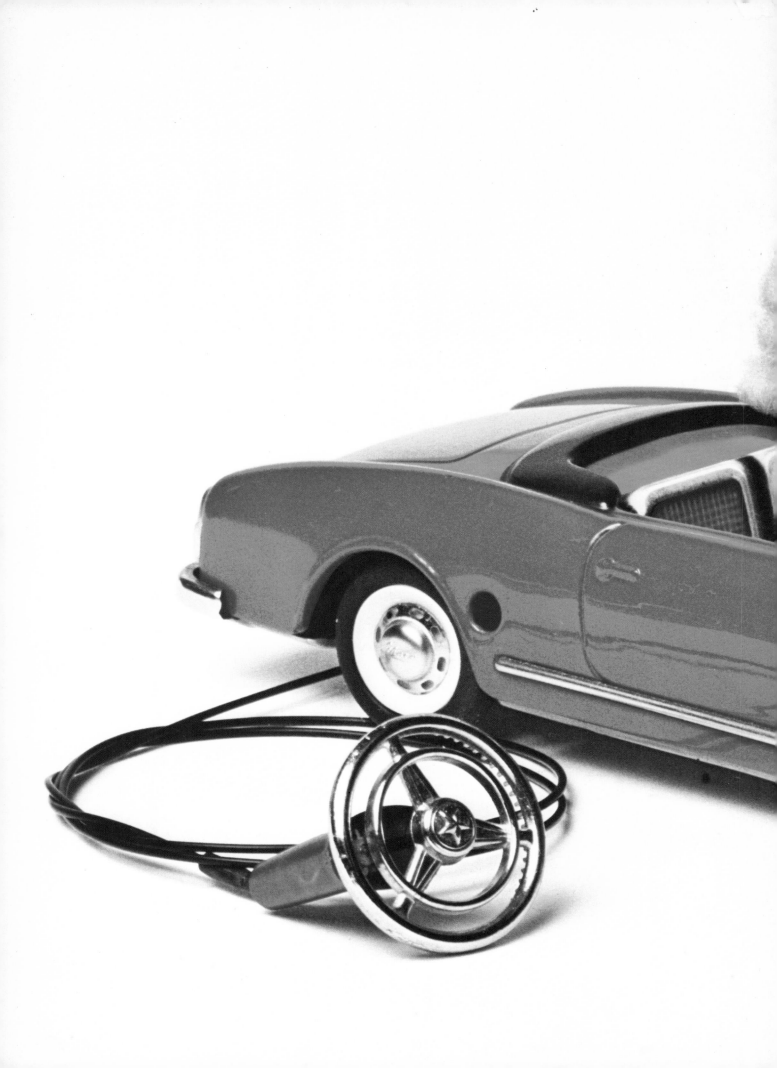